From Cutlasses
to

"Liverpool Police Force is composed without favour of the best men that can be picked, it is directed by an unusual intelligence."

Charles Dickens, 'The Uncommercial Traveller'.

"The police and public must win this fight against crime as a combined operation, otherwise life for all sections of the community becomes fearful and miserable."

James Haughton, 'Report of the Chief Constable to the Liverpool and Bootle Police Authority for the year, 1967'.

From Cutlasses

to

Computers

The Police Force in Liverpool
1836-1989

by
W. R. Cockcroft

Foreword
by

Sir Kenneth Oxford

S.B. Publications

This book is dedicated to my wife and children.

First published in 1991 by S.B. Publications
Unit 2, The Old Station Yard, Pipe Gate, Nr. Market Drayton
Shropshire TF9 4HY

British Library Cataloguing in Publication Data
Cockcroft, William
From Cutlasses to Computers:
The Police Force in Liverpool (1836-1989)
I. Title
363.20942753

ISBN 1-870708-46-6

Typeset and printed by Delmar Press (Colour Printers) Ltd., Nantwich, Cheshire
Bound by Manchester Free Press, Jersey Street, Manchester M4 6FP

CONTENTS

ACKNOWLEDGEMENTS

The author wishes to record his gratitude to those many members of the local police service who by their selfless devotion to public duty have made this record of their achievements possible.

He particularly wishes to thank the following for their help and individual expertise so vital to the preparation of this book:-

Sir Kenneth Oxford.
James Sharples, Chief Constable of the Merseyside Police Force and the members of his Police Authority.
Tony Mossman, Merseyside Police Press and Publicity Officer
The staff of the Liverpool City Library
Margaret Caulfield
Brian Dolan
John D. Robertson
Peter Woolley
Steve Benz of S.B. Publications.

THE AUTHOR

William Cockcroft was born in Liverpool and has lived in Merseyside for most of his life. After graduation, with honours, from U.C.N.W. Bangor, he was subsequently awarded a Masters Degree in History, and advanced diplomas in the teaching of Mathematics and Science. He has recently completed twenty-five years in education as both teacher and lecturer. His interests include supporting the Friends of the Merseyside Maritime Museum and the Botanic Gardens Museum, Southport. He has recently completed two additional books due to be published in the near future: '*Liverpool's Dangerous Historic Docklands; The Albert Dock Heritage*' and '*A Dome of Fire; Fire-Fighting in Liverpool, 1836-1990*'.

FOREWORD

by Sir Kenneth Oxford CBE QPM DL

The concept that people should be responsible for law and order within their own community pre-dates the Norman Conquest in the 11th Century but it was not until 1829, with the passing of the Metropolitan Police Act, after years of parliamentary vacillation, that the foundations were laid for the 'New Police', a regular Police Service as we know it today.

Until 1829, law enforcement was lacking in organisation. Although the office of Constable had existed in one form or another since the 13th century, the personnel were too often corrupt, untrained and ill equipped to deal with the increasing lawlessness which accompanied urban and industrial growth, particularly in a vibrant, volatile and thriving seaport such as Liverpool.

The success of the 'New Police' was quickly recognised by parliament and in 1835 the Municipal Corporations Act was passed requiring provincial towns to organise their policing in a similar fashion to London. Few towns complied with the legislation, but of those which did many were undermanned and inadequately trained or equipped. Liverpool however, known for its sense of civic responsiblity, was an exception. The proportion of police to population in Liverpool was unequalled and in 'general efficiency and discipline' the Force was unsurpassed by any similar establishment in the Country.

William Cockcroft has written a fascinating historical survey of the devlopment of the Liverpool Police (ex parte Merseyside), a development that continues to this day — always in the vanguard of technical development; sensitive to, assisting with and adapting to social change.

It has been said that total freedom is anarchy, total order tyranny. The Police, who represent the collective interests of the community, are the agency which holds a balance somewhere between; a concept which is not happily recognised by some political ideologies. Their standing is a rough index of society's own attitude towards the regulation of civilised living; regard for the police, which should not of course be uncritical, is regard for law and order. I have always felt that complaints against police were complimentary of the police ideal and the service as a whole — a paradoxical view to some.

Anyone who reads this admitted brief history will soon realise what a colourful and varied existence the Liverpool Police have had. Difficulties there have been, of that there can be no question. Some are of their own making but in the words of the author. . . 'They police the localities of Merseyside, efficiently, compassionately and with insight and intelligence. Liverpudlians and indeed Merseysiders can be justly proud of their local guardians of law and order both past and present'.

There is a dearth of historical research about the Liverpool Police and William Cockcroft's admirable and informative work has made a valuable contribution to remedy that. Surely there must be another book waiting to be written if only to satisfy the historical interest engendered by this one.

I was privileged to serve with the Merseyside Police and to experience personally, without equivocation, the loyalty and integrity of all members. In consequence, I read this book with great interest coupled with a deep pride in the great Force about which William Cockcroft has so ably written.

PREFACE

When the Liverpool City Police Force was amalgamated with the Bootle Borough Force, 1 April 1967, an era in Merseyside police history had passed. For over a century many far-sighted people had fought for a smaller number of police forces in Britain; many still seek a 'national' constabulary.

Whatever the benefits of a uniform system of police might be, amalgamation marked the end of the remarkable record of the Liverpool Police Force, which began in 1836. In general terms, the men who composed this body had helped establish standards of law and order which could hardly have been conceivable when the Force was first founded.

In this small book I hope to give Liverpool citizens — and all who cherish law and order — some idea of the splendid achievements of the Borough 'bobbies' together with those of their successors, the Merseyside Police.

Part One

INTRODUCTION

THE CITY OF LIVERPOOL

Liverpool, a busy commercial city with a population numbering more than three-quarters of a million people by the second part of the twentieth century, is situated on the east bank of the River Mersey. It is a seaport of international fame and boasted at its peak more than seven miles of docks. Many of the latter in the nineteenth century and early twentieth century were capable of receiving the largest ships afloat.

As the home of a large cosmopolitan population, the city itself is extremely popular with tourists and has trading traditions that link it to many parts of the world. Efficiently accessible — through a series of arterial routes, to a busy hinterland — it became noteworthy for its local, modern industries such as motor-car assembly, glass making and light engineering. It remains a proud and vigorous City, displaying a variety of attractive facilities including its museums, university, cathedrals, theatres and association football clubs.

It developed, therefore, not solely as a port. Inside an area totalling nearly 30,000 acres, its business and shopping centres rapidly expanded, as did the industrial and residential suburbs which extended into open countryside. Several of its housing estates have become characterised by popular T.V. programmes as containing a unique brand of 'native humour'. In many other spheres, too, Liverpool is now regarded as a fashionable tourist centre and a progressive city.

Having recently rediscovered the attributes of a thriving city, it has the added advantage of good communications to all parts of England, Wales and Scotland, by rail and road, and to Ireland and the Isle of Man by sea, or air.

Present Merseyside police constables will agree that from recent experience, the city is still both interesting and difficult to patrol. It covers a large portion of their territory and has a huge population and since it is still occupied with commerce it has enormous volumes of traffic.

These and other factors create serious problems for the police in the protection of life and property, the control of crowds and the direction of traffic. Especially difficult problems have traditionally arisen with the supervision of valuable merchandise at the docks and in the warehouses.

The vital importance of Liverpool was shown by its development as the chief point of departure for European emigrants in the nineteenth century. During the Second World War it received near fanatical attention from the enemy. It is true to add that few cities in the British Isles today, can boast as exciting a tradition of local policing, as Liverpool can.

THE FORMATION OF THE FORCE, 1836

Liverpool was so vile and wicked a port in the last century that it was known as the "Black Spot on the Mersey". International visitors agreed with this description because of the terrible social conditions in the dockland districts and the city centre. Brothels, bawdy theatres, gin-palaces, penny ale cellars and thieves' lodging houses in their hundreds, sprang into existence in the first half of the nineteenth century.

Ideally situated and offering exceptional facilities for maritime trade and passage, the port expanded alarmingly. It became a magnet for workmen from all parts of Britain and from Ireland in particular. Many, who later stayed, saw it as the "Gateway to the West", or the springboard to a new life in the British Colonies or the United States. Between 1801 and 1831, the population more than doubled, while from 1831 to 1841 there was a further increase of 80,000. This 'boom' period reflected itself in the eight new Liverpool docks built between 1815 and 1835.

Hence, it was hardly surprising that the old parochial organisation of the port began to collapse. Piece-meal provisions for health, education and law and order became completely inadequate, for the new large population.

Fortunately, the Liberal Council of 1836 decided that the three independent constabulary forces — the Corporation Constabulary, the Town Watch and the Dock Watch — would have to go. This was hardly surprising, since these constabularies had terribly low standards of health, education and general organisation. They fought among themselves and the dock watchmen regularly attacked the town watchmen and locked them overnight in their dock-side bridewells. One Captain Morrow was described as a typical town watchman, "he sometimes breaks out drinking and continues it for two or three days — on those occasions he reports himself to be suddenly taken ill."

Town and dock watchmen were notorious for their heavy drinking bouts. They regularly fought each other, accepted bribes and deserted their beats — In contrast the 'new police' in their distinctive uniform were better organised.

3

Equally corrupt, were the corporation constables, members of a small day-time street force who regularly accepted bribes and deserted their beats. One was carried off to Ireland, by mistake, in a drunken condition. The town watchmen, too, became infamous for their rash drinking, brawling and their bullying of citizens on Saturday nights.

When sober, the watchmen only patrolled as far as the parish boundaries. In 1833, for example, four watchmen were responsible for Toxteth Park and Harrington, where 25,000 people lived. Hence, in these and in the other outlying townships, such as Everton and Kirkdale, gangs of ruffians and thieves lived solely by crime.

Few respectable citizens, therefore, were satisfied with the unsurpassed criminal activities carried on in the town both by day and by night. Reckless seafarers from all over the globe, together with thousands of thieves, prostitutes, vagabonds and juvenile delinquents crowded into the dockland areas and those insanitary parts of the town nearest them. Here, numerous receivers of stolen property, brothel-keepers and managers of beer-houses and beer taps earned a steady income. In 1836, for example, more than 1000 known male thieves lived in the town, whilst 500 others "stole at intervals". Some 600 more operated at the docks and upwards of 12,000 children, less than fifteen years of age, worked as thieves for adults.

Drink was easy to come by, many distilled their own liquor, and beer and public houses stayed open for most of the day, "It appears that there are between three and four hundred public houses in the Borough, that are habitually kept open until after twelve o'clock at night and from 900 to 1,000 that are open on Sunday morning before four and six o'clock and remain open until church hours."

Liverpool's centre, was indeed a hot-bed of illegal activity. Williamson Square may be taken as an example. Over 100 brothels situated near the Square, could all be seen in a fifteen minutes' walk. In one nearby street alone there were no fewer than twenty two. In these and the rest of the town's 300 'known' brothels, wines and spirits were always on sale. Four prostitutes, on average, or 1,200 prostitutes in all, lived in these houses. More than double that number lodged elsewhere. Many of these women, moreover, supplemented their earnings by assisting notorious thieves who cohabited with them.

Their children, together with thousands of others — abandoned, neglected or homeless — roamed the streets, and became feared for their acts of savagery. Like many of their mothers, they had primarily turned to law-breaking, more from necessity than choice, but once convicted they soon became hardened criminals. It has been estimated, in fact, that over 15,000 children living in Liverpool in 1835, did not attend school.

Liverpudlians, however, were not unique, for such scenes of disorder and deprivation were common to other large British towns. Just outside the Borough, along the Lancashire and Cheshire coastlines, inland between the town's outskirts and those of the townships of Kirkdale, Everton, West Derby and Toxteth, and on the Liverpool to Manchester roads, many people earned their living by breaking the law. In Cheshire, many coastal inhabitants deliberately planned shipwrecks and entire villages turned out to join in the spoils. On the canals leading out of Liverpool, too, thieves had their own special depots for the reception of canal cargoes.

Needless to say, therefore, something drastic had to be done to protect Liverpool's law-abiding citizens. The bodies of men responsible for the Town and Dock watchmen made a start by recruiting outstanding officers from Sir Robert Peel's Metropolitan Police Force, in 1830. Lieutenant Parlour, himself appointed in this year brought the entire Metropolitan Police arrangements to Merseyside and these were kept to form the basic structure of the Liverpool Police Force, formed in February, 1836.

Welcoming the powers vested in them by the Municipal Corporations Act, 1835, the newly elected Liberal Council — with John Holmes, J.P., a prominent Liverpool merchant playing the key part — formed the new force together with Michael Whitty, the first Head Constable.

Using the Metropolitan plan, Whitty separated the town into two main police divisions; he divided them by drawing a boundary line on the town map from Water Street, along Dale Street, up Shaw's Brow and directly to Low Hill. His men were to use the Exchange Street East Bridewell and Vauxhall Road Bridewell as their northern headquarters; in the south they used Brick Street Bridewell and the Duncan Street North Bridewell. He then subdivided each Division into eight sections. To each of the former, he appointed a Superintendent and inspectors took charge of the sections.

For the first 360 policemen, however, conditions were terribly harsh; the constables, even in the most inclement weather, did an average of twelve hours duty per day, without any day of rest. For their toil they received a mere eighteen shillings per week. Some of them even had extra duties to do as town firemen.

The Merryweather 'steamer' Livingston.
Two of the fire-engine maintenance crew are pictured, in 1898, attending to the steam fire engine, Livingston. This Liverpool horse drawn vehicle, capable of delivering 460 gallons of water per minute at the fire face, is seen in Bradewell Street at the side of the Westminster Road Fire Station.

5

Liverpool City Police Fire-engine Crews.
Several steam fire-engine crews and their principal officers gather at the central fire station, c.1890.
Their headquarters was at Temple Court before the new Hatton Garden fire-station was opened in 1899.
The Merryweather steamer shown was eventually capable of delivering
1,600 gallons of water per minute.

Part Two

CRIME

CRIME IN LIVERPOOL

We cannot fully measure the threat of the Liverpool criminals to law and order at any given time. We cannot be sure of the precise number of crimes prevented by the police, nor can we estimate the exact number committed during a certain period. Liverpool's criminal statistics, prepared and issued between 1836 and 1967, covered only those crimes 'known to the police'. The tables thus only give an estimate of the number of crimes committed.

It would appear that the best judge of police efficiency was the reaction of the public to the type of service and protection they received. This, too, had its defects, particularly in the nineteen sixties when our modern urban police forces were seriously suffering from a shortage of manpower.

What cannot be denied, however, is that Liverpool policemen have had to face some remarkable threats to the safety of the town. When the first constables stepped out to patrol the town, as we have seen, they faced almost overwhelming dangers from the juvenile delinquents, the prostitutes and the drunkards; crimes of violence were high — knives, bludgeons and other dangerous weapons were used freely and the street brawl was an accepted way of settling disputes. On a much grander scale, many dissatisfied townspeople perpetrated outrages during the General and municipal elections and the Orange and Catholic communities waged unmerciful war against each other. As the century grew old, open violence began to recede but still flashed to the surface in the serious Fenian attempts to disrupt the public peace. They almost succeeded in their aims to blow up the Liverpool Town Hall and a police constable's residence in Dale Street.

Liverpool's juveniles continued to be a cause of great public concern even in the twentieth century — particularly during the two World Wars and right up to the nineteen fifties when the famous Juvenile Liaison Scheme began to have an effect.

General public dishonesty, too, appears to have grown. From the nineteen thirties onward, larceny, in the aggravated forms of burglary and house-breaking seems to have become the bane of Liverpudlians. Thus, these crimes seem to have kept pace with the remarkable growth of population and property.

During the 'fifties' and 'sixties', Liverpool folk began to hear and read more and more about new and alarming types of crime. Organised 'London style' robberies came to the fore. These were made notorious by the increased planning and determination of the criminals. Hence, larcenies involving large sums of money — often gotten by attacking commercial and private transport — became the main feature. In 1965, for example, almost half the total recorded Liverpool crime related to petty theft, much of which, Chief Constable Haughton believed, could have been prevented "if the owners of the property had taken reasonable steps to safeguard the items stolen." Four thousand, nine hundred and twenty thefts were from unattended vehicles, 894 thefts of bicycles, 605 thefts from automatic meters, 1,864 thefts from shops and stalls and 4,813 minor and miscellaneous thefts. It would appear, therefore, that the Liverpool police were caused unnecessary trouble by Liverpudlians and others who carelessly 'tempted' persons to commit crime.

So what types of crimes have caused our city constables their greatest concern?

JUVENILE DELINQUENCY

Liverpool juvenile delinquents have always kept the city policemen busy. In 1966, for example, 2,263 juveniles came ot their notice for criminal offences; of these 1,728 were prosecuted and the other 535 were cautioned. These young people, and the boys in particular, would have posed an even greater problem if it had not been for the Liverpool Juvenile Liaison Scheme, introduced by Chief Constable Charles Martin, in 1951. James Houghton recorded some remarkable statistics in his 1966 chief constable's report. Of the 12,946 children supervised since the scheme was introduced, some 2,570 became involved in further offences, giving an overall per cent of 19.85% recidivism.

Liverpool folk, however, can be thankful for the gradual reduction of the problem over the years. The town's first policemen had to face thousands of ill-clad, ill-fed, homeless and unemployed children plaguing the public places, streets, thoroughfares and entries of the port. Often having abandoned home, they soon acquired a precocious knowledge of adult bad habits. Their first misdeed was usually to steal pence from the shelves, drawers or even from the persons of their own parents, to obtain food or admission to some low theatre or fair. Late hours, loose associates, abandonment of home, robbery from person and shops, and utter vagabondism would follow in succession.

Hundreds of these children regularly lounged about at the coarse town theatres, such as the 'Sanspareil', the 'Liver', the 'Queen's Theatre', the 'Custom House' and the 'Penny Hop' in Hood Street. Visiting the latter in 1841, Captain Williams, Her Majesty's Inspector of Prisons, was shocked to discover, "the streets and avenues leading to it occupied by crowds of boys. It consists of a spacious room fitted up in the crudest manner, with a stage, and seats on an inclined plane, — the access to it is through a dark passage and up a ladder staircase. On one occasion I was present, I found the audience to consist almost exclusively of boys and girls, of the lowest description, many without stockings."

Crowds of these poor creatures flocked to the low fairs when attracted by their gaudy facades. They particularly went to see the coarsely presented scenes of crime and bloodshed. "The Murder of Maria Martin in the Red Barn," by Corder, or "Hannah Brown" by Greenacre, were especial favourites. Other managers showed schools for thieves, with a host of lessons in villainy.

Even twenty years after the Force was founded, such places were plentiful in Liverpool. Amongst others there was the Williamson Square Free Concert Room, the Lord Nelson Street gambling halls, the Royal Casino near the docks, the Salle de Danse theatre, and several pugilists' and dog-fighting and rat-fighting public houses.

Many children lived solely by stealing from the thousands of shop-keepers and street-traders who recklessly exposed their property. In and around the public places nothing was sacred; ropes, pairs of trousers and stockings, cuts of beef and ham, waistcoats and quantities of sugar were all taken. Hundreds of town pawnbrokers accepted dubious goods without question and perpetuated this flood of petty larceny.

Until the middle of the last century, these offenders, once in court, were sentenced to punishment similar to that of adults. Even for stealing food, they were sent to prison. Once inside, they were regularly whipped or fettered in solitary cells in the Kirkdale

County Prison or the Borough Gaol in Howard Street.

In 1847 an Act was passed to ensure the more speedy trial of juvenile offenders and to avoid the evils of their long imprisonment whilst awaiting trial. This was accomplished by giving the magistrates power to deal with simple cases and to limit the sentences to three months' imprisonment. Some Liverpool boys found their way into industrial schools, being sent there by the magistrates on a 'free pardon', conditional on attendance. Others were sent to the 'feeding schools', variants of the industrial schools, where they were given some education and training in a trade. Liverpool's young offenders were sent as far afield as the Philanthropic Institution, Surrey, the Dalston Refuge, Middlesex, as well as to the County Refuge, Chester and the County Refuge at nearby Edge Hill. Other reformatories included the Clarence and Akbar training ships anchored in the River Mersey.

By the middle of the century, there had been further improvement. In 1854 reformatory schools, which had been established by voluntary enterprise received recognition and were given grants and subjected to Home Office inspection. After this year courts could sentence a boy to detention in such a reformatory.

By this time the industrial schools, which had been established principally for destitute and vagrant children, were subject to Home Office inspection. Magistrates were authorised to send to them children found begging, or wandering without homes, frequenting the company of thieves, or beyond the control of their parents and there they might receive a rudimentary education.

At the same time, Liverpool policemen began to notice the civilising influence of the "Ragged Schools" and other schools in the worst neighbourhoods of the City. This was important for, apart from the hostile attacks on people — such as the indiscriminate stoning of Liverpool churchgoers — the delinquents continued to pillage property. Many of them attended thieves' schools for 'professional' tuition in pocket-picking and grand larceny. Thus, the Chairman of the Watch Committee readily sanctioned the use of City police in securing returns for the Liverpool School Board, which was established in 1870.

The police constantly made attempts to remove children from the sources of crime. They sought legal powers to visit brothels and remove the children, including the very young females, living at such premises. However, their efforts were not always appreciated and 'wild charges' were made against them. The 'Liverpool Review', 22nd August 1885, for example, alleged that dock constables had freely used canes and sticks against "wretched, half-starved and ragged children."

During the last twenty years of the century police work for needy children was extremely commendable. They sent boys and girls found begging to the Islington Children's Shelter, where food was paid for them by the Watch Committee. They efficiently enforced the Prevention of Cruelty to Children Act, of 1889, and the legislation to protect children from licensed premises and street trading. Chief Constable Nott Bower, welcomed these efforts at a time when "the dirt of the delinquents, the swarm of vermin, and possible disease", made disinfection of child prisoners a very difficult task for his men.

Realising the difficulties experienced by the orphans of former policemen, too, he helped found the Liverpool and Bootle Police Orphanage, which opened in 1895, and eventually acquired a large house and grounds in Woolton.

Some of the ragged and barefoot children commonplace in Liverpool, c.1895.
In the 1890's newspaper headlines such as that shown were widespread.
The popularity of gambling activities is also depicted by the 'sports results'
on the wall posters behind the drink-carrying boy.

The magnificent efforts of the constables to look after deprived Liverpool children did not rest here. In a single year, 1895-96, the Liverpool police-aided Clothing Association inquired into the cases of 4,532 insufficiently clothed children. Members of the Force had initiated the society and managed it in the 'nineties, to collect and provide money, boots and clothing for children. They particularly helped the dock-side children, many of whom depended on parents dogged by unemployment, drunkenness and other reckless habits of life.

The distinguised work of the Police Force continued into the twentieth century. This is not to say, however, that the constables had an easy task when confronting the juvenile delinquents. During the two world wars, the threat from these young people was severe. Nevertheless, the police made a serious effort to provide differential treatment for juvenile offenders. They were kept apart from other prisoners, confined at the Belmont Road Workhouse instead of in the police cells, and were especially conveyed to court and tried at special times. By the Children's Act, 1908, no child under fourteen years of age was to be sent to prison, and a juvenile over fourteen could only be sent if the court was satisfied he was too unruly or depraved to mix with other juvenile delinquents. Those awaiting trial were to be kept apart from other offenders. Remand Homes were established in which the juveniles could be kept until their case had been dealt with in the new juvenile courts. Ordinary members of the public were excluded from the latter and further privacy was guaranteed by prohibiting the publication of information which might identify those juveniles appearing.

Many were of the opinion that birching kept down the number of juvenile delinquents. In fact, in 1915, 350 juveniles were birched. Nevertheless, during the Great War offences of dishonesty, particularly by young persons whose fathers were away from home, showed a steady increase. Offences against property with violence, by juveniles apparently increased, too, after the war. To many onlookers, the persistence of the offenders suggested that the methods of dealing with them were not effective.

Later, the Children and Young Persons Act, 1933, as amended by the Act of 1935, extended the principles of the 1908 Act, for children under twelve, to all those under seventeen years of age. The Court was to have regard to the child's welfare in dealing with it and was, in a proper case to take steps for providing for his education and training. The distinction between reformatory and industrial schools was done away with and both called 'approved schools'. Other methods of dealing with juveniles, such as the use of a foster home, or supervision by a probation officer, was made available in some cases. The 1933 Act also gave increased powers to remove from their homes, children who were in need of care and protection.

Liverpool Education Committee acquired Penketh School, near Warrington, in 1938, to supersede the Hightown Approved School. This new school was noteworthy for its modern facilities, including an open-air swimming pool, gymnasium, workshops and plenty of open land. Girl offenders were sent to Derwent Road Remand Home, Old Swan.

In spite of these facilities, however, juvenile delinquency in Liverpool, at this time was about three times as great as that in the county of Lancashire. Approximately three-quarters of the offenders came from an area representing about one-quarter of the City — the inner districts bounded by Kirkdale Ward in the North, through Netherfield ward, Low Hill ward and Abercromby ward, to Toxteth ward in the south. Many parts of the outer town districts were almost free from juvenile delinquency. The only outer districts infected, seemed to be the new housing estates. Such offenders seemed to act mainly after school time, particularly on a Sunday, when they raided unoccupied premises.

Those probation officers supervising the delinquents were greatly handicapped by their own shortage of personnel and accommodation. Lack of employment opportunities for the young was a key root cause and it was felt "that many of the urchins who throng the courts and who are often regarded as the foes of society are, in reality, its victims, requiring assistance rather than punishment."

With the outbreak of the Second World War the situation apparently became worse. By 1945, the cases of "breaking in" had increased 300% on that of the pre-war level. Indictable crimes committed by juveniles in general increased by up to 25% Thus this surge in crimes coincided with the depletion in the Liverpool Police Force, and the recruitment of many Liverpool fathers and teachers for war service.

Though the presence of police officers, especially appointed in 1949 to work in connection with the prevention and detection of juvenile offences, led to reduced numbers of young offenders, it was however, the Juvenile Liaison Scheme which led to a remarkable improvement.

Chief Constable Charles Martin introduced this invaluable scheme, in 1951, to invoke the assistance of all those interested in the welfare of young children to prevent juvenile miscreants from committing offences. The most important people in this respect were the parents of the children concerned. After a child was cautioned, the police, were mainly occupied with giving advice to the parents and the child.

The children were mainly those, under seventeen years, who had committed a minor offence such as petty theft. Once they admitted the offence, and if they had never come to the notice of the police before for being in trouble, their parents were approached and asked to co-operate with the police by accepting the latter's advice about the child's future. Following the introduction of the scheme, managers of the larger city stores — formerly plagued by swarms of children seeking a chance to steal, reported a great drop in such incidents — Large reductions of theft were also reported by the market store-holders, and the guardians of the nut-treating mills and sugar refineries. In 1953, in fact, only 1,508 juveniles were prosecuted for indictable offences — the lowest recorded in the previous sixteen years.

Under the provisions of the Criminal Justice Act, 1948, an attendance centre for Liverpool was established at the Wellington Road Boys' Secondary School. Later it moved to the Gordon Working Institute. Here, a chief inspector and a voluntary panel of sergeants supervised the boys between 2 p.m. and 4 p.m. each Saturday afternoon.

In 1963, centres at Mather Avenue and Nile Street were opened. The boys were first paraded for a general cleanliness inspection and then the policemen divided them into groups for different types of instruction, which included woodwork, plaster modelling, physical training and handicraft instruction.

By the mid sixties, Liverpool juvenile offenders were receiving vastly different treatment from the imprisonment, whipping and transportation procedures which the first police constables had to witness. So famous, moreover, had the Liverpool Juvenile Liaison Scheme become by this time that police officers came from forces in the United States, Germany and further afield to personally examine it. This interest stemmed from Chief Constable Martin's invitation by the United Nation's authorities to bring detailed information about his scheme and to speak about it to a congress on the prevention of crime and the treatment of young offenders in Geneva.

DRUNKENNESS

Public drunkenness never caused our modern police constables the trouble it had caused their predecessors in the last century. Nevertheless, excessive drinking in Liverpool merits a close look because it often led to terrible crimes of violence against both citizens and policemen. The latter never accepted their own statistics for prosecutions as a clinical measure of public sobriety; the people arrested were only those drunkards 'known' to the police. Many who became drunk in private were obviously never arrested by the police. The problem confronting the police changed over the years, too. In 1836 excessive widespread public drinking concerned the Force. By 1967, young people, obtaining their drink from 'private' sources became the main problem.

The town in the nineteen sixties was a far cry from that in 1836 when public houses, beer houses, taps, gin palaces and penny-ale cellars existed in their hundreds. Known thieves kept about ten public houses and known prostitutes about the same number. Some forty cheap singing saloons became the rendezvous for the town boy and girl urchins. An idea of the excessive number of liquor palaces is reflected in the fact that without moving from a certain point, not far from the Vauxhall Road Bridewell, in 1830, it was possible to count twenty-seven public houses and beerhouses.

Little could be done for many years because the law and business interests did little to prevent drunkenness. Early Tory-dominated city councils favoured the brewer interests and often forced the chief constables, via the Watch Committee, to safeguard the public house licences. In 1847, for example, a publican, with a friend on the Council, stormed into a local police station and threatened to take a certain constable's coat "off his back" if he dared to prosecute him. The Liberals on the other hand were often bigoted and took little heed of police experience in their zeal for temperance. Thus, the police were sometimes seriously handicapped by the local magistrates. Head Constable Greig exacerbated the antagonism between the licensees and his Force by using some of his men in plain clothes. In 1857, one magistrate, under pressure from the brewers, dismissed several informations laid against beer-shop keepers solely because police officers had made 'plain clothes' visits to the premises.

With the encouragement of the brewers, many Liverpool magistrates felt free, in 1862, to grant licences for public house drinking facilities to any persons showing themselves to have 'suitable premises'. By 1866 some 336 beerhouses had become licensed in this way and were added to the already excessive total. This experiment collapsed in the latter year but only after many known thieves and prostitutes took over licensed premises.

Worst afflicted appeared to be the dock labourers who had to live close to their source of work — the docklands abounding with public houses. Many stevedores fell to the mercy of the 'lumpers', who accepted a major job for a lump sum of money and then sub-contracted it to them. If the labourers did not accept the lumpers' prices and treat them to free beer on 'paynight', they lost favour.

In 1830 an Act of Parliament permitted free trade in beer — any person whose name was on the rate book might open his house as a beer-shop free from any Justice's licence or control, merely on payment of two guineas to the local office of Excise. In Liverpool alone, there opened more than fifty additional beer-shops every day for several weeks, and by the

14

end of the year the total number of licences granted in England and Wales rose to 24,342. It was hardly surprising that a vigorous Temperance Movement spread throughout the country; the David Jones Society, established in Gay Street, Scotland Road, in January 1835, was among the first branches of the movement.

Undoubtedly, in such circumstances, the liquor problem caused the Liverpool Police Force their biggest headache for years. Fortunately, after much trouble, the Intoxicating Liquor Licensing Act, 1872, helped improve the situation — it necessitated amongst other provisions, that public houses be managed in a better fashion. The town's streets became quieter by night, and especially on Saturdays. After this Act, the sale of intoxicating liquor was restricted to between 7 a.m. and 11 p.m. on weekdays and to between 1 p.m. and 3 p.m., and between 6 p.m. and 9 p.m. on Sunday, Christmas Day and good Friday. Employers, consequently, found fewer men absent from work and many citizens were delighted as Sunday mornings became more peaceful.

In spite of this improvement, some Liverpool folk were still far from satisfied and joined together to form the Liverpool Vigilance Committee in 1875. Unfortunately, the extremists of the Committee became obsessed with an urge to increase the number of convictions for drunkenness and pressured the Head Constable into increasing his public house inspection corps. Greig's special inspection branch was well organised — with uniformed inspectors and constables in plain clothes visiting the licensed premises — but the scheme was costly and time consuming, taking experienced men away from more important duties.

Greig's successor, Nott Bower was totally against the system feeling that the area falling under this scheme was too large for such a comparatively small group of eleven men. His determined efforts brought the censure of the temperance party upon his head. Fortunately, the Watch Committee did not share their views and allowed him to abolish the special corps and make his superintendents responsible for supervision in their Divisions.

Following this, the police began to witness a decrease in public drunkenness. Nott Bower adjudged this development had occurred not only because of his new strategy, but also because of the increasing scrutiny of the licensing magistrates, the clearance of large pockets of unhealthy living accommodation in the oldest districts of the seaport and the destruction of the living quarters of many infamous law-breakers. He added to these factors the trade recession in the early nineties, the inadequate wage levels, the growth in the popularity of organised sports such as football and cycling and the better modes of getting to and from work (whereby men were able to arrive at their destinations without stopping at the beer outlets). Finally, he believed the termination of the 'subbing' of wages (whereby pay clerks allowed workers small advanced amounts), the greater stringency of the benefit societies concerning those men who drank in excess and the closure of many drinking dens had significantly affected the overall situation.

The police recognised, however, that the reduction in prosecutions for drunkenness could not be taken as a safe index of a proportionate increase in temperance. When many people were prevented from becoming drunk in Liverpool's public places, they began to carry drink away from the licensed premises and to get drunk elsewhere. The police were pleased, however, to see that each year the demand for a higher standard of public behaviour seemed to increase. They also recognised that though they arrested more people for drunkenness, following the 1902 Licensing Act, it did not mean that more Liverpool people were becoming drunk than previously. It merely meant that the new legislation regarded those found 'drunk' and incapable of looking after themselves as now liable for arrest.

Greater attention was now paid to the habitual drunkards and the movement to treat such people as ill, rather than as criminals, began to grow. Hence, the Church of England Temperance Society informed the Head Constable, in 1900, that they intended to establish a certified reformatory for the reception of inebriate women under the Inebriates Act, 1898. If they were deemed incurable, Liverpool Women were sent to the Lancashire County Council Reformatory at Langho. As the move for female emancipation developed, public opinion became increasingly directed against the deplorable amount of drinking by women.

Stricter attention, too, was paid to the condition of licensed premises and following the Licensing Act, 1904, many insanitary beer houses opened before 1869 were closed. It is interesting to note, that when the area of the town in 1904 was much smaller than that in the nineteen sixties, there were 2,020 licensed premises in the former year and yet by the latter period the number had fallen to 1,282.

The police also witnessed an unbridled growth of gambling at licensed premises. Chief Constable Sir Leonard Dunning felt that the Street Betting Act, 1906, drove betting practices from the streets into the licensed clubs. He noticed that the 'working classes' in particular were spending more money on betting and the football pools than previously. Nevertheless, slum clearance schemes and the new practice of house to house delivery of beer bottles by holders of licences led to increased sobriety in public places.

With the end of the Great War, 1914-18, the improvement continued but a new and notorious feature of the drinking problem was the growth of methylated spirit drinking among the poorer people of the Port. General conditions, however, continued to improve, especially with the widespread attempts by the townspeople to enjoy an 'open air' life by making use of the motor coach, railway excursions and by using bicycles.

Between the world wars, and particularly in the 'thirties, the Borough Police became alarmed by the spread of slum clubs. Many, they discovered, were structurally unsound, insanitary, and were run by book-makers, solely for drinking and betting. They became notorious for the excessive drinking, foul language, and the grossest obscenities practised in them between men and women. For many years, the constables had great trouble in curbing their menace because they were easily registered and opened and usually introduced elaborate precautions — such as 'spy holes', electric bell warning systems, barbed wire and heavy iron doors — to keep out the police.

Fortunately, the Force was able to tackle the problem and witnessed, by constrast, during the Second World War, 1939-1945, a remarkable decrease in drunkenness. The cost and scarcity of wine and spirits, the reduced alcoholic content of beer, earlier closing times at public houses, staff shortages therein, and a curtailment of Liverpudlians' spare time, did much to produce this effect. The number of shebeens, or private houses, where a room was set apart for drinking purposes — drink being sold at higher than normal prices — did increase. Customers were usually of foreign nationality, however, and their numbers began to decline after the war.

From this time onwards the problem of drink seemed to move increasingly away from Liverpool's public houses which in general became managed with very high standards. More and more attention became focused on drunkenness among young persons and on those adults driving motor vehicles whilst under the influence of drink. The 'sixties, in particular, were notorious for the escalation in all forms of gambling. By 1965, for example, there were 242 licensed clubs in the City and 507 betting offices. Chief Constable, James Haughton, noted the concern being felt by members of the public about the numbers of the licensed clubs in the city centre advertising 'gaming until dawn'. Wisely, he had his men maintain a careful watch on the position knowing that it is very often as a result of such activities that crimes of violence are committed. This type of business, too, he held, tended to lend itself to the institution of protection rackets and although some allegations were made, he found nothing to prove that these existed in Liverpool.

Public attention, at the same time began to focus on drug trafficking. Here, too, Liverpool police officers — and especially the Vice Squad — were continually engaged in preventing any serious developments. Young people were regularly watched, particularly in the various clubs and cafes in the city centre, where transactions were possible. The preventive aspect of police work was emphasised by the fact that officers made some 448 visits to 217 chemist shops, in 1965, in connection with the enforcement of the Dangerous Drugs Act.

Hence, the character of the Liverpool drink problem had greatly changed over the 130 years of Liverpool police history. Unfortunately, some of the features, such as the drunken attacks on members of the public and police officers continued with tragic consequences.

PROSTITUTION

Together with drug trafficking, the Liverpool police Vice Squad, centred at 'A' Division headquarters in the City Centre, concentrated on the city prostitution problem. The Squad was formed in 1964 in an attempt to offset the difficulties experienced by plain clothes personnel from one division going into another to pursue enquiries. Before its formation there had been no common policy in the methods for dealing with such information. Two years later, the inspector in charge, his four sergeants and sixteen constables in the Squad, affected 124 arrests of prostitutes and adminstered cautions in 236 cases; five women were charged with controlling prostitutes and 23 males were charged with living on the earnings of prostitution.

Though in the 'sixties the prostitutes still constituted a serious menace, it was small compared to that of the previous century. Street walking prostitutes in the experience of our modern constables, usually only solicited those males whom they thought were looking for their services, whereas previously many women depended for their very existence on their trade and openly procured payment by any male. Nevertheless, the latter day prostitutes by their habits encouraged men to kerb crawl in their motor cars in certain districts of the town and many respectable female students, nurses and housewives complained about their being approached in such a fashion.

In general, however, the prostitutes did not command the abhorrence of respectable Liverpool citizens as they had done in the nineteenth century, when they were as much a political issue, at the time of the municipal elections, as was the liquor problem. The dockland was flush with the sailors of many nations in the 'thirties, 'forties, 'fifties and 'sixties — Yankee clipper seamen, Liverpool-Irish 'packet rats', 'China Birds', and West Indian and West African negroes — and these made several areas of the port infamous for soliciting. In 1836, for example, there were an estimated 300 known brothels and about 1,200 known prostitutes. The port, too, was very much smaller than the modern town.

These women primarily plied their trade in the sailors' quarters, which spread from Lancelot's Hey and its surrounding alleys and rows, through Castle Street and its back streets from Wapping to Park Lane and Paradise Street, reaching as far as the lower end of Pariament Street and its neighbouring side-streets. They eventually moved as far into the port as Lime Street in the very heart of the City.

Such females were but one of the money raising sources of these seamy quarters. The low theatres, singing saloons and fairgrounds offered overwhelming chances of cheap sensuous relaxation. There were also people in Liverpool who kept houses for boys and girls who wished to live together in promiscuous intercourse. With the town offering the most depraved forms of entertainment, including dog-fighting, rat and badger-baiting, the nearby Borough Gaol in Howard Street, and the Kirkdale County Gaol, became the receptacles for disgusting human beings. The Inspector of Prisons, in 1837, found women in the Howard Gaol "creeping alive" with vermin. Ten years later, little had changed, for he found women in prison "lying like pigs doing nothing. . . in gaudy clothes, torn and soiled with blood and dirt, the effects of drunkenness and quarrelling. Gonorrhoea and syphilis, were common among such inmates.

Liverpool was not alone in this respect, for together with Glasgow, Bristol and Bath, it became one of the most notorious centres for prostitution outside London. Many young girls, and in particular the children of the immigrant Irish, were forced by the shortage of work to take to the streets. According to Captain Williams, H.M. Prisons Inspector, of those committed for prostitution from 1 January to 30 September, 1864: 605 were of Protestant upbringing, whilst 921 were Catholic. Many such women he found, though not more than 26 or 27 years of age, had been in gaol between thirty and sixty times.

In their attempts to tackle the problem, Liverpool policemen were handicapped by the law. For many years they could only charge these women if they were found causing annoyance to others. The brothel-keeper, too, could only be prosecuted if he kept a disorderly house. Provisions for prostitutes, at the same time, varied from town to town in Britain. Some cities, mainly those where there were military camps, were subject to the Contagious Diseases Act, 1864, and rigorous checks were levied against suspected prostitutes — Liverpool was free of this law and the numbers of those following this way of life increased almost unchecked. In 1861, the Liverpool police knew there were 686 practising prostitutes in the town; ten years later, their numbers had increased to 764.

So openly and so unashamedly did these women solicit that their scandalous behaviour was raised as a political problem.

There was hardly a respectable Liverpool home where the matter was not discussed. Some people, like Josephine Butler, attacked the problem as its roots and attempted to improve the social and economic conditions which gave rise to the problem. Others tried to force the Police to prosecute indiscriminately and have the severest punishments introduced for such practices.

Josephine Butler and her husband began to take outcast women into their own home when they arrived in Liverpool. She sought to improve the lot of those in the Liverpool Workhouse and developed her campaign into a national one for the moral purity and the abolition of the degrading Contagious Diseases Law. Writing articles and pamphlets and addressing meetings of protest she was sometimes sympathetically received, at other times with ignominy and violence. Some Liverpool merchants supported her and helped her, in 1867, to establish an industrial home for homeless females. They appointed a matron to manage the house to ensure the girls learnt laundry duties or the work involved in a small envelope factory.

It was with such merchants and their friends that the Liverpool Temperance Party originated. Though many of its supporters wanted sweeping reforms to remove the ill-repute attached to the name of Liverpool — several extremists failed to consider the practical methods of achieving reform. Thus, from time to time, the notoriety of Liverpool prostitutes caused the greatest friction between the Head Constable and the Temperance Party. Urged on by their vociferous temperance supporters, the Liberal Party fought a series of municipal elections on the questions of vice.

In November, 1890, when the Liberals won the control of the Council, Chief Constable William Nott Bower, was forced against his own experience to follow their orders. They argued that because it was an offence to keep an immoral house, the police should prevent any such house existing and that constables should "clear the streets of prostitutes". Though Nott Bower and his predecessor John Greig had, by close supervision, gradually reduced the number of brothels to 443 in 1890 and confined them to certain districts — thereby preventing them from spreading — the Liberals wanted all known brothels closed. Nott Bower vehemently opposed this policy because he knew from experience they would always exist for the large seafaring population and an attack could scatter the brothels into respectable districts or even force the prostitutes into the open streets, alleys and passages of the City.

As a direct consequence of the Liberals' policy, the police laid a total of 443 informations against Liverpool's known brothels. Their action aroused public indignation, it caused extreme harshness among the women concerned and, in general, restricted positive reform. It did much to spread the evil into respectable neighbourhoods and among innocent people. In the new areas the brothels became difficult to supervise and the police often found it difficult to obtain evidence against them. His men noticed many more prostitutes using common lodging houses, entries, passages and other places to which the public had ready access. It was fortunate that, in 1896, a special council committee was formed to face the whole question. Consequently it recommended a return to the pre-1890 policies.

The twentieth century witnessed the continuation of the improvement. That is not to say that moral standards improved, but that prostitutes carried on their work without openly breaking the law as frequently as before. The improved means of communication, especially the early spread of electric trams, transported the nuisance to suburban areas and in many instances beyond the City boundaries, especially on the Cheshire side of the Mersey. Those using houses of accommodation did so with the utmost care and it became increasingly difficult to get information and evidence, especially in the suburbs where the beat constables became fewer. A further feature was the increased number of brothels kept by foreigners, many of whom became engaged in robbery. About the same time the police began to notice the spread of lewd and objectionable literature in the form of cheap books, newspapers and post-cards.

Once again, public attention became increasingly focused on the movement for improving the status of women. Hence, there were calls for the provision of decent hostels for single women for while Liverpool men had the Bevington Bush Hotel and the David Lewis Hostel, in the early years of the present century, the women had none. Perhaps one result of this inadequacy was the fact that it encouraged the 'privateer' or amateur prostitute, who met in parks, or other public places, with chance acquaintances.

The Great War saw no acknowledged increase in prostitution — though large numbers of young Liverpool girls were attracted onto the streets in the neighbourhood of military camps. The decline of street soliciting was due largely to the bands of voluntary women patrols which were formed under the auspices of the National Union of Women Workers, with the sanction of Chief Constable Francis Caldwell, in November 1914. By 1918, the organisation was receiving a small grant of £100 and had opened an office in 5 Cases Street. Two years later, the women opened a much needed hostel for young women in Old Swan.

These precautions were necessary in Liverpool for there was an increasing tendency for irresponsible, careless and ill-mannered young women to preen themselves and visit public houses and places of amusement, solely to tempt men to treat them to drink or refreshment or entertainment. This menace particularly acute during the Second World War when

Lime Street Station became recognised as the meeting place for girls, sometimes from outlying towns, who came into the City to 'pick up' members of the Allied forces. The Chinese and foreign eating houses in the south end of the City, too, also attracted young women and encouraged them to discard their identity cards or ration books. Miss Winifred Todd Pratt, a former director of the Women Police Patrols, felt that unlike the Great War when girls of seventeen and eighteen years were the problem, the Second World War saw girls as young as thirteen and fifteen years of age claiming they were eighteen.

On the 31st December, 1947, the Women Police patrols ceased to function and City Policewomen Corps was established. This branch of the Force began to carry out invaluable tasks, under-taking duties in all divisions; working with the C.I.D., Crime Prevention Department, Juvenile Liaison, and Traffic Departments (including the Information Room, the Motor Patrols and Road Safety department).

By 1966, members of the Policewomen Corps were affecting nearly 1,000 arrests per year. Probably their most important duties became those connected with tracing girls under seventeen years reported as missing from home — some 653 girls, in fact, in 1966, were reported to them in this connection and by the end of the year only seven had not been traced.

The nature of female crime had greatly changed during the history of the City Force. Social and economic changes and the wisdom of police policy had helped to reduce prostitution and enable Liverpool citizens to concentrate their efforts on improving the moral welfare of young women. In this latter respect, our city policewomen carried out work of inestimable value.

Women Police Officers, 1951.
This branch of the Liverpool City Force
undertook invaluable tasks in all divisions.
They assited the C.I.D., the Crime Prevention
Department, Juvenile Liaison and,
as shown here, the Traffice Department
with road safety duties.

MAINTAINING THE PUBLIC PEACE

When the Liverpool Football Team returned with the F.A. Cup on Sunday, 2nd May, 1965, and paraded from Lime Street Station to the Town Hall, crowds of more than one hundred thousand taxed the resources of the Liverpool Police Force to its limit. Chief Constable James Haughton, moreover, was perturbed that many of the mounted police horses had their forelegs bruised by kicks from teenage girls wearing pointed shoes; the 'mounties', it would appear, had prevented the girls from running into the middle of Lime Street in front of the team's coach. Blameworthy as these girls were, it was a sign of the respect that Liverpool people had for their Force that no other serious damage occurred. Such respect, however, has been hard earned by the Force when it has saved the City, at various stages in its history, from being plunged into complete chaos.

Michael Whitty, the Town's first head constable, had one of the most difficult tasks in establishing and preserving the public peace. During his term of office he had to regularly face all the evils of angry mobs and factions antagonised by the stress of living under terrible economic and social conditions. Catholic and Orange hatred for each other was intense, the Corn Laws roused thousands of Liverpudlians to bloody demonstrations and there was a tradition of mob violence in the port at the general and municipal elections. Some 20,000 people, for example, attended an Anti-Corn law Association meeting held in Clayton Square, in June 1841. Whitty had to conceal 300 men in nearby St. John's Market in preparation for any disturbance and though he managed to prevent any serious trouble near the Square, mobs of Irish labourers moved off and started a series of attacks — lasting for two days — on their enemies. This was by no means the end of his troubles for a short time later in the Summer of 1841, he had to rescue the town from disaster during a parliamentary election. Whitty's own account, recorded in the Watch Committee Minutes, Vol. 2, 3rd July, 1841, speaks for itself:

"My men were occupied without intermission, in pursuing the most desperate mobs, armed with every kind of weapon, and dispersing dense crowds of curious and idle people.

It was not until 6 p.m. when the turbulence subsided that the mounted policemen and their horses were sent to rest and eat. This lull was only short lived.

Immediately after seven o'clock, Mr. Superintendent Riding sent me a mounted policeman to say that the state of the south end demanded my presence with a reinforcement. The men instantly remounted and I thought it right to arm them with cutlasses. I ordered Mr. Superintendent McDonald to send fifty men after me, but the state of the north end was such as to render it prudent to deny him compliance.

On my arrival in Saint James Street, I found a mob of at least twenty thousand persons, several gentlemen vociferously urged us forward exclaiming that they were murdering the people. The word 'people' sounded to my apprehension like 'police', I ordered the men to draw their cutlasses, but cautioned them as to their use, except in a last extremity, and then galloped through the mob, which precipitately fled. Just emerging from Greenland Street I met a strong body of police with Mr. Superintendent Riding, James Lawrence Esq., a member of the Committee was with them. Both exclaimed against the special constables who had by their conduct increased the disturbance.

It appeared that on their way from the different south polling places they had stopped with Mr. Riding and on the very unexpected commencement of the rioting about six o'clock he took them out with him. Discovering, however, their inutility and something worse, he was in the act of putting them into Saint James' Market when I came up. I kept them there until twelve o'clock at night lest they might, if sooner let out, create a disturbance themselves, as they also had been fearfully excited.

While clearing St. James Street my attention was attracted to the park. In Grafton Street the lower classes of Irish, and those who are religiously and politically opposed to them, and who reside very numerously in the neighbourhood had come in contact; they amounted to several thousands, many of them formidably armed. We charged them successively and prevented, I am disposed to believe, the loss of life and property to an incalculable extent. The Irish fled to the neighbourhood of New Bird Street, Crosby Street, etc. and I placed two sections between them and their opponents, who at first appeared rather daring, but on being repeatedly charged, fled too.

From the arrival of the mounted police, no outrage took place and it is due to the horsemen, to say, that they did not inflict the slightest injury on a single individual.

In the meantime frequent alarms were given of outrages principally the breaking of windows in Park Lane and the streets leading into it. Many of them were groundless, but too many were true. and to prevent their recurrence, the whole body of police was kept constantly moving in detachments.

They were everywhere attacked, and an attempt was made to assault the horsemen with stones at about half past nine o'clock in Mill Street, but, having anticipated them by quietly introducing two sections on foot, the party got a good beating and the streets soon after became quiet.

In the course of the evening a very melancholy occurrence took place at Salthouse Dock, some persons attacked the house of Mr. John Casement, a licensed victualler and ship's carpenter by trade. They demolished his windows and he fired two pistols loaded with shot. Three lads and a girl were wounded, but none, it is hoped fatally, the whole transaction is described as having occupied only a minute or two."

By Thursday evening the ferment subsided, and the men resumed their ordinary duty. The conduct of the police during a three day period was as can be seen exemplary.

As more and more Irish flooded into the town, conditions worsened. By the mid '40s they were swamping the lodging houses, the workhouses and the bridewells. In the shabbiest districts, brawls and bouts of fighting occurred with great frequency and only the constables' actions prevented a never-ending cycle of bloody violence. These conditions led to a nervous time for the Town authorities and they anticipated a serious clash with

Chartist supporters in 1848. They called in the militia, had the police drilled in the use of cutlasses and had one hundred picked men trained with carbines. However, they were not called upon; nor were a small number of Lancashire policemen, mounted and armed for the occasion, in the outskirts of the Town.

The increased numbers of Irish intensified the antagonism between the Catholic and Orange communities and March 17th, St. Patrick's Day, and July 12th, the Anniversary of the Battle of the Boyne, usually saw the police prepared for the most serious demonstrations.

During the same period, the dockland districts bred violence on a grand scale. An ever increasing number of steam vessels brought more sailors for shorter visits, and the toughest type of characters sailed in with them. Quayside violence, especially stabbing cases, gave Liverpool an evil reputation by the middle of the century. Until the mid 'sixties the majority of visiting sailors carried sheath-daggers and engaged in drunken brawls and fits of fighting. In 1856, the yearly total of recorded stabbings had been as high as 185 and yet the dock policemen were often unable to prevent such offences because they were mainly committed by persons of the lowest class of society when drunk or in a sudden passionate rage.

The dock quayside also became the arena for numerous larcenies as valuable merchandise was carelessly left on them for long periods. So troublesome did these thieves and others become that in 1865 a River Police Department was formed to help cope with them. In the main, the small section of about twenty men, was to prevent 'crimping', or shanghaiing on the River Mersey and at the pier-heads.

They were badly handicapped, for years, because they only had three small rowing boats allocated for their use and these 'gigs' were frequently involved in accidents. In 1868, the

The River Police Launch, 'Argus', c.1912.
Liverpool's river policemen, were principally occupied, after 1865, in preventing 'crimping' for the sailing ships on the River Mersey. For more than thirty years they had to row, or sail, small gigs on the river. In 1895, they managed to visit 3,608 vessels in the Mersey but greatly welcomed the use of a steam launch in 1899. Their acquisition of the 'Argus' reduced their risk of an accident while afloat.

constables of a capsized boat were only just saved by the two Mersey lifeboats. The strength of the Mersey tides, even during fine weather, was often too much for the men. As late as 1875, the River police had to depend on the goodwill of masters of ferry steamers for a tow in the River — against a tide of upwards of six miles an hour. By the 'nineties, however, crimping had largely disappeared as a Merseyside practice and Nott Bower agitated for the termination of the section.

On land the Borough constables had to constantly deal with new dangers threatening public order. In the eighteen forties, for example, the influx of large crowds into Liverpool on a Sunday caused great concern. Many strangers, from outlying districts, began to flock into the Town, using the new cheap railway services. They caused undue excitement, bustle and inconvenience in the Borough. On 13th July, 1845, 5,300 trippers arrived at an early hour in the morning from Manchester. A week later, 7,000 journeyed from the same town and caused the main roads and passageways stretching from the Edge Hill railway Station to the pierheads to become dangerously overcrowded. From the early morning hours until midnight large groups of these travellers boarded the vessels sailing to the Mersey Light Ship and back.

Organised strikes, too, presented a particularly serious problem to the Force. When the dock labourers struck, in February 1879 for example, the local militia had to be called in. Such economic distress was perhaps only to be expected in a city containing a high proportion of unskilled labour. Large numbers of German and Italian immigrants swelled the ranks of the unemployed and the tempestuousness of several Liverpool districts. In times of hardship they joined any impulsive demonstrations such as the Liverpool bread riots in 1850.

Nor were the Liverpool Irish protests confined to movements demanding higher wages and shorter hours. Chief Constables Greig and Nott Bower, in particular, faced the dangerous Fenian outbursts. Greig's prudent action in speedily dispatching information which came to his notice, in February 1867, prevented violent Fenian attacks in both Chester and Dublin.

Greig witnessed the climax of their violence in Liverpool, in 1881, when they attempted to destroy the town hall and the Hatton Garden Police Section House. Their bomb did explode in the lobby of the section house, a residence for young constables; although considerable damage occurred this was restricted to the opening passageway of the house. This was daring, since many constables were in the section house, it adjoined the town's principal police station and a large number of constables were patrolling the adjacent streets. Only the great courage and resourcefulness of the policemen — and especially Constable Reade — on duty in the locality of the town hall, saved the fine old building from damage.

His successor, Nott Bower, maintained the public peace with equal effectiveness. When it was alleged in a series of Liverpool newspapers in 1886, that dangerous and highly organised bands, or High Rip Gangs, as they were popularly termed, had been formed, he quickly investigated the accusation. The 'Liverpool Review', in July, reported that a quasi-secret society, formed for the purpose of plunder and violence on dock labourers, executed vengeance on all in 'D' Division who ventured to give evidence against them. The scare continued, until Justice Day put an end to it. He, together with the second assize judge, Justice Grantham, were taken on a tour of the Division by the chief constable. The two men were appalled by the extreme poverty, squalor and drunkenness in the district. At the November Assizes, in 1886, Justice Day scathingly referred to the absurd stories afloat about the High Rip Gang. The Calendar showed a great number of robberies with violence and as each verdict was brought in, he ordered that the prisoner await sentence until the last day of the Assizes. On that day all the prisoners were brought into the dock for sentence, and each of them (in addition to the term of imprisonment) was sentenced to be flogged, with twenty or thirty lashes of the 'cat'. This was carried out in two instalments, the second immediately before release from imprisonment, to give the prisoners' acquaintances opportunity to witness the result. It was soon apparent that the sentences had a dramatic effect in this locality.

For many years, however, public behaviour left much to be desired. Chief Constable Leonard Dunning, in 1903, lamented the continuing sectarian strife between Catholics and Orangemen. In that year, for example, following an open air religious meeting, crowds of bigots had gone so far as to stop tram-cars on which their protagonists were travelling, and they had assaulted passers-by. During the first decade of the twentieth century, the mere sound of a drum from one of these communities caused serious outbursts of violence. At such times free use was made of stones and bricks and the war-cries of 'Paddy is a bastard' and 'Billy is a bastard', regularly rent the air.

As P.J. Whaller has so skilfully chronicled, by 1909 Liverpool had become a city embroiled in a 'sectarian civil war'. Official authorities, including the police, all had their own explanations for the outrageous bigotry shown by both sides. Whatever their interpretation might have been, the behaviour of both the Catholic and Protestant communities perpetrated lasting traditions of hatred and mutual mistrust.

In 1909 it would appear, hostilities resulted from each side attempting to better the other by public demonstrations of the fervour of their faith. On 9th May, for example, the Catholic Holy Cross Church diamond jubilee led the celebrants to erect an open air altar in the Marybone district. Leonard Dunning accepted the promise of the processionalists not to carry and display their Communion Host and to use only those streets that were in the Catholic districts. In these the papal coloured bunting, the outside services of the Stations of the Cross and the processional walks came perilously close to the Protestant Chapels.

At the same time Dr. George Wise, the celebrated leader of the Protestants — a professed anti-infidel lecturer against disbelief, 'including popery' — marched on the same day as the Catholic parades. Inevitably, at the Catholic wayside altars — and all except that approved at Marybone were illegal — disturbances broke out.

Within the next two weeks Dunning's request for restraint was totally ignored by both communities. When the Head Constable was on holiday on 20th June, members of St. Joseph's Catholic Church undertook yet another march. Orangemen for their part planned to resist what they believed was an illegal procession and they assembled in Juvenal Street despite the presence of seven hundred policemen in the locality. Scuffles broke out, fifty five arrests were made and these precipitated the beginning of Liverpool's 'Civil War'.

A new dimension of 'terrorism' quickly followed as houses were marked to denote their occupiers' religious creed. Beatings and lootings signalled the struggle to shape the

Netherfield and Scotland areas as the respective bastions of the two faiths. In one week alone, 130 convictions for offences against property and 81, for violent assaults were recorded. Liverpudlians, in their hundreds moved out of their homes to 'safe houses'.

Further shocking incidents of terrorism and intimidation ensued as gangs strove to establish denominational supremacy, whether in street or work place. The sectarian inheritance of this period thus became a semi-permanent legacy to Liverpool's main religious communities in the decades that followed.

The situation improved little before the Great War, and afterwards, in 1921, the situation became so severe that the police engaged on certain duties had to be armed; as Chief Constable Caldwell pointed out 'on several occasions armed offenders narrowly escaped being shot'.

Before the Second World War, trade depressions and disputes also brought a tremendous amount of extra work for the Force. In 1911 strikes extended practically over the whole year and during the general strike of the transport workers detailed below, in Chapter 22, the Chief Constable had to look for assistance from outside Liverpool and eventually from the military and special constables for the protection of property, and especially goods in transit through the City. August was a particularly bad month in this year, a very serious riot occuring in Lime Street on 'Bloody Sunday', 13th, whilst an open air meeting was taking place on the plateau of St. George's Hall.

On 15th, an attack was made in Vauxhall Road on a prison van and in its defence, by the military, two men were shot.

An open air meeting on the plateau of St. George's Hall, 'Bloody Sunday', 13th August, 1911. An estimated crowd of 90,000 gathered to hear various speakers supporting the transport workers' strikes.

In 1918, the arrival of American troops caused much extra work and the sinking of the Lusitania in 1915 had caused such an arousal of public feeling that many unreasoned attacks were made upon the persons and property of those who appeared to have German connections and affiliations.

After the First World War, too, the slump in trade and the growth in unemployment led to a government drive for economy. In spite of the government's gestures of reconciliation several strikes brought the threat of still more, between 1919 and 1921. A distinct change in the trade unions' attitude was noted after mid 1919.

With the coalminers' strike still unsettled the fever of unrest burst out afresh in Liverpool and in other British ports. Some citizens feared revolution was approaching as even Liverpool City Police members appeared to them to be fanatical as they went on strike. The seaport's branch of the National Union of Police and Prison Officers, with many ex-servicemen in their ranks became determined to stand by their principles and to risk their jobs and pension rights.

A confrontation between the Liverpool Watch Committee and a large majority of the City police force was emblazoned in headlines in the local newspapers, 1st August 1919. As shown below, in Chapter 23, they followed other members throughout England and Wales, who were members of the Police Union.

The Watch Committee in turn issued its ultimatum that every police officer who did not immediately return to work or parade at his divisional station for orders at 8 p.m. on that day would be dismissed and on no account be permitted to rejoin.

For his part Head Constable Francis Caldwell warned the public that he would not be able to protect property as before, and he appealed to householders, shop-keepers, warehouse and other business owners to take their own steps to safeguard their property.

Within hours, the effects of the impasse were stunning. Troops from the Nottingham and Derby and South Staffordshire regiments came in by the lorry load to be billeted in tents in St. John's Gardens, at the rear of St. George's Hall. Looters appeared as night fell in the nearby Byron Street and adjacent Scotland Road districts. The attacks by men, women and youths of both sexes on a number of shops caused widespread damage and considerable quantities of goods were taken. By August 4th photographs in the local press depicted scenes outside the Owen Owen Emporium showing all the windows on its frontage smashed. Armed soldiers on guard outside of Messrs Bachelors Big Shop appeared, too, as did tanks 'in readiness' on St. George's Plateau.

In this sequence of events the Battleship Valiant and two destroyers steamed up the River Mersey and a fleet of government lorries arrived to move food supplies and to prevent congestion at the docks and railway stations. Across the river in Birkenhead, quantities of boots, drink, tobacco and groceries were stolen before the Riot Act was read and some fifty three persons, including women, were arrested.

Those sent for trial in Liverpool for alleged shoplifting or being in unlawful possession of stolen goods amounted to some three hundred and seventy. Many offered no defence other than that 'they picked up the goods in the street'.

Once convicted their sentences ranged from 6 weeks to 3 months' imprisonment. One man found in possession of a single boot and a coathanger, of no use to him, was fined £5. Yet another, Cuthbert Howlett, a boiler makers' labourer was 'justifiably shot dead', in Love Lane, during the disturbance.

The ability of the local authorities to react in such rapid fashion had been achieved partly by the use of the troops — some 2,500 in total — and partly by the use of 730 special constables quickly enrolled. Their response, too, was also helped by their widespread newspaper advertisements for new recruits to join the police force. Thus 'New Chums' in the familiar City police uniform soon appeared at the commencing wages of £3.10s. per week and the promise of a pension.

Those policemen who did strike suffered immensely. After their dismissal they were all refused reinstatement and they forfeited their pension rights. With labour unrest being widespread in this difficult post war period, alternative sources of employment became very scarce.

In contrast the preparedness of the police to meet the calls and emergencies during the General strike, 1926, and the local and national arrangements for securing the maintenance of the supplies of essential commodities, greatly contributed to the preservation of public order. The anxious period was during May when widespread stoppage of industry took place. Beyond a few isolated instances of intimidation or assault, little occurred in the nature of threats of violence to life or property.

Following the financial crisis of 1931, the City was remarkably free from any serious disorder. This was not the position, unfortunately during the Second World War. Liverpool became a 'number one' port, between 1939 and 1945. Many British ships were diverted here from their home ports and many foreign ships brought cargoes here; it also became a reception centre for refugees. At one period there were a number of serious incidents at dance halls, stemming from the friendly treatment of coloured servicemen from the U.S.A. When Chinese and other coloured people also began to associate with white women serious incidents occurred, necessitating the formation of a special police mobile reserve of picked men. The presence of men with money and time on their hands, as we have seen, attracted loose women from all parts of the country and led to the establishment of houses of an undesirable character. In spite of the 'blackout' difficulties, however, the police were able to cope with the brothels and the 'shebeens', or illegal drinking houses.

After the war, fortunately, there were few examples of serious public unrest — except for the anti-Jewish riots in 1947, when two British soldiers were hanged in Palestine and in 1955 when Strikes involving the dockers, railway men, seamen and tugboat-men stretched the resources of the Force.

From this time, especially during the 'sixties, with the shortage of manpower, the Force faced its greatest difficulties when any large crowds assembled. Hence in 1964, the regular visits to the City by well-known local "pop groups" attracted large crowds of young people but effective police measures were taken to control them.

The most unique visit of this type was on 10th July of that year, when a civic reception was given to the Beatles, followed by the Northern Charity Premier of their film "A Hard Day's Night". This visit strained police resources to the limit due to the unprecedented crowds it attracted but only a few incidents of a minor nature occurred.

Something of a 'trend' was established by this visit because the following year the visit of members of the Royal family and large numbers of people congregating in the vicinity of various city theatres in connection with performances by the 'Rolling Stones' and the 'Beatles' caused police leave to be cancelled on a large scale. After this there were numerous sporting occasions demanding a police supervision on a grand scale: such occasions included the Grand National race-horse meetings at Aintree, the F.A. and Football League triumphs of both Liverpool and Everton and the great influx of visitors for the World Cup matches at Goodison Park on 12th, 15th, 19th, 23rd and 25th July 1966. During the latter period, in fact, all police leave was cancelled. One match, on 12th July, coincided with the procession of the Loyal Orange Lodges and this necessitated the Chief Constable switching constables rapidly from Goodison to the City centre. Thus members of the mounted police department did invaluable work as they had done at fifty-seven football matches played at the Liverpool and Everton grounds, in 1966, when a total of over two and one half million spectators attended.

Part Three

THE ORGANISATION
OF THE FORCE

Merseyside Policeforce Area Map, 1974.

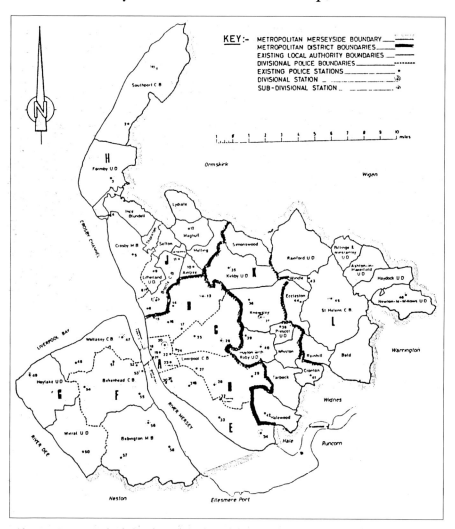

KEY:- METROPOLITAN MERSEYSIDE BOUNDARY
METROPOLITAN DISTRICT BOUNDARIES
EXISTING LOCAL AUTHORITY BOUNDARIES
DIVISIONAL POLICE BOUNDARIES
EXISTING POLICE STATIONS
DIVISIONAL STATION
SUB-DIVISIONAL STATION

Other Stations: Rainford Road, Rainford; Robins Lane, Sutton; Thatto Heath Road, St. Helens; Clipsley Road, Haydock; Billinge.

Boundaries: The whole of the Metropolitan District of St. Helens.

Petty Sessional Division: St. Helens. Divisons A to E cover the approximate territory of Liverpool City Police Force (before amalgamation with Bootle Police Force which formed part of J Division) in 1967.

POLICE DIVISIONS

Some of the principal officers of the City Force, 1898.
The Fire Brigade, the Band and the Mounted Police are among those represented here,
possibly prior to a full inspection in Sefton Park.

Dividing the town into two Divisions, in 1836, and copying the Metropolitan organisation of the Force, Chief Constable Whitty established the pattern of the later organisation of the force. As the area to be policed by the Liverpool Force increased, further Divisions were added. Nott Bower reformed the Force into five divisions in the eighteen eighties. By the nineteen sixties there were seven territorial divisions.

Those constables working in 'A' Division were mainly responsible for the central borough area where the city's chief business and shopping centres were situated. Since the western boundary was the River, they also patrolled the main landing stages for cross-river ferries and ocean-going passenger liners and the docks used by the Irish steamers.

Covering approximately 650 acres, it was the home of a comparatively small residential population of about 15,000 people. During the day, however, the transient population and the traffic were enormous and in addition to the commercial importance of the division, all the principal theatres, cinemas, hotels and criminal courts and the Liverpool entrance to the Mersey Tunnel were situated therein.

'B' Division, by contrast, with its headquarters at Prescot Street, was almost entirely an industrial-residential area. The property in it, in the main, was old and the houses were nearly all of the terrace type. Three of Liverpool's main arterial roads passed through the Division and daytime traffic was extremely heavy. Some 108,000 people lived in the Division, which was a relatively small area of 1,600 acres.

Like 'A' Division, 'C' Division also adjoined the River Mersey. It, too, was mainly an industrial-residential Division, served by its Lark Lane Police Station, but its property varied more than that in 'B' Division. With 74,000 people living in an area of about 1,135 acres, 'C' Division which included extensive docklands and the main installations of the Port of Liverpool, was a very busy place for the police.

Rose Hill Police Station was the headquarters of 'D' Division which had previously been one of the toughest in the Town. Covering approximately 800 acres, its population was originally immense and most of the worst types of dwelling-houses were here. Extensive slum clearance, however, had by the 'sixties considerably improved the Division and reduced the population to about 36,000 people. Mainly residential in character, it also included many docks used by coastwise steamers, and a large number of very large industrial installations. The main road out of Liverpool to the North passed through the Division and presented a considerable burden to the police with its heavy daytime traffic.

'E' Division also demanded close police supervision. Parading at Westminster Road Station, the constables on duty witnessed a variety of change in the 4,180 acres of the Division stretching from a dockland of warehouses and factories, near the River Mersey, to the modern suburban area of great housing estates near the city boundary.

The Division took in all the largest docks of the port of Liverpool, including those in the Borough of Bootle. Thus the supervision of these docks and the handling of the enormous quantities of transport to and from them presented to the police some of their most important duties. The men were also fully engaged safeguarding a large population of 128,000 people, the crowds at Liverpool's two main football grounds and the Aintree racecourse.

Largest of all the Liverpool Divisions, stretching across 12,850 acres was the 'F' Division, with its headquarters in Ganworth Road, Speke. Bounded on the west by the River, there were no docks to supervise, but the men had 202,000 people, living in a variety of residential property to protect. They were also responsible for Liverpool Airport, a large factory development and the large Corporation Housing estate at Speke.

The final Division, or 'G', had its headquarters at Eaton Road, and covered 6,720 acres. Police Constables serving here were also responsible for a large residential population of some 180,000 people. With several of the busiest of Liverpool's main roads passing through it, its property varied widely from the industrial area adjoining 'B' Division to the suburban area near the city boundary.

These seven police divisions formed the natural basis of the organisation of the Liverpool Police Force. Most of the Force's personnel were engaged on uniformed duty within these divisions, but a City as complex as Liverpool required many other duties and responsibities for the police, which were dealt with in the various departments of the Force separately administered from the division headquarters.

At the same time, two departments, comparable in strength to the seven Divisions, operated over the entire City. These were the Criminal Investigation Department and the Traffic Department.

A Chief Superintendent was responsible for the former and for each complete C.I.D. staff which was attached to the seven territorial divisions. In addition, the Crime Squad, dealing with major crime, operated throughout the City.

Liverpool had had a detective department from the very beginning of the Force and it had performed invaluable work. A Flying Squad, composed of experienced detectives who assisted the uniformed men of the various divisions when they investigated serious crimes, had operated in the Town since 1924.

Unfortunately, the C.I.D. could not always be kept up to strength. Although, by 1965, crime in the City had increased two-fold within the previous ten years, the overall depleted strength of the Liverpool Police Force meant that detective officers had to undertake excessive caseloads to combat the influx of crime.

The Superintendent in charge of the Traffic Department was responsible for the operations of all mobile patrols, the general transport of the Force, wireless communication, road safety, hackney carriage supervision and the Information Room.

Liverpool traffic policemen had first patrolled the town's roads, in 1920, by motor-cycle combination. Before this time horse-drawn patrol wagons had been used but there had been no particular department to supervise them. The traffic department began their motor car patrols in the 1930's. Ever aware of the increasing menace of road traffic, Chief Constable Charles Martin established a Road Safety branch of the department in 1949. Responsible for the compiling of road accident statistics, the furthering of road safety measures among the community, particularly the children, the section appointed and administered the School Crossing patrol personnel.

Police Motor Cycle Patrol.
Liverpool traffic policemen first patrolled, in 1920, by motor cycle combination.
The Royal Enfield Winnipeg special, registration number CKD 13, was capable of exceeding 70 mph.

A two-seater, early sports style City police patrol car.
The officer in the passenger seat is seen operating the radio equipment fitted behind the front seats.
The vehicle, c.1935, an M.G. tourer bears a Liverpool registration ALV 52.

An idea of the scope of the work of the members of this section is to be gained from the fact that in 1965 they dealt with 1,877 cases of reckless, dangerous and careless driving, 4,990 excessive speed offences and they supervised some 264 men and women employed as School Crossing Patrols.

So heavy had road traffic become by the 'sixties, moreover, that on midnight, 7th May, 1966, a one-way traffic scheme had to be introduced in the city centre. The plan included seven main routes on which the traffic signals were linked by means of master controllers to enable traffic to flow through the city centre at twenty to twenty-five miles per hour. The new system appeared to work well, though one 'breakdown' in the Mersey Tunnel often paralysed large areas in its vicinity. With some 17 million vehicles a year using the Tunnel, the potential congestion from such breakdowns was considerable. Nor was there much hope of immediate improvement when work started on the second Mersey Tunnel in January of the same year.

When the Liverpool Force was amalgamated with that of Bootle, 1st April, 1967, Chief Constable James Haughton introduced a more modern approach for the structure of the new force. This he did, keeping in mind the developments in communications and the changing road, traffic and crime patterns. He introduced much larger divisions to replace those of the former Liverpool Force, and a separate command became responsible for the whole of the Dock Estate. Each new division, moreover, had the same structure for rank.

WOMEN POLICE

In the nineteenth century the influence of local women on the policies of the Liverpool police force was very restricted. Though many females were arrested for a wide range of crimes they could usually only look for support to a small group of wealthy lady volunteers. These included in their ranks the remarkable Josephine Butler. Such brave helpers as the latter often had to face a torrent of verbal abuse and physical harassment, rather than any degree of sympathetic co-operation, from many males. This entrenched antagonism retarded the employment of female labour in the police service until the middle of the twentieth century. Those who continued to press for a change of attitude to the employment of women constables had to wait until the crises of the two World Wars of the twentieth century significantly altered the role of women in our society. Liverpool's bands of voluntary women patrols, with their Cases Street headquarters, particularly helped to improve the plight of needy local women between 1914 and 1918. Prominent members of the patrols, such as Miss Winifred Todd Pratt, an eventual director of the women's police patrols, helped highlight the growing city dangers to young women in war time.

Her work and that of her helpers would appear to be all the more remarkable because, at a national level, the story of women's involvement in police work, was one of apathy and prejudice, until after the Second World War. Women constables, most police authorities felt, were an unnecessary and somewhat extravagant luxury. Few chief constables, unlike Liverpool's Leonard Dunning and Charles Martin, valued their contribution to police work. Again, it was only after the Second Great War, that they became recognised as an integral part of their force.

Women Police Constables, c.1950 in Church Street performing traffic duty.
In spite of the inclement weather conditions they admirably control the pedestrian crossing
before the installation of a 'Zebra Crossing'.

Dunning, in the first two decades of the twentieth century, had a remarkably modern outlook with regard to the need to employ women. For him

'a woman by advice and personal influence can do more than a man to protect a girl from temptation of her own nature. . . there is a definite place for women in the police force of any place where those temptations are many'.

Liverpool, undoubtedly, has many such temptations throughout its torrid life as an international seaport.

As we have seen above, the Liverpool women constables, from the time of their introduction, in 1949, had invaluable work to perform, particularly in those cases concerning women and young children. The first entrants, drawn from many walks of life, still had to face — as did many of their successors —the undisguised malice and vindictiveness of many men within our society.

THE MOUNTED DEPARTMENT

Mounted Policemen, c.1897.
These splendidly attired officers await inspection at the annual parade before H.M.I. of Constabulary
in Sefton Park. Their military bearing and distinctive uniform owed much to the standards set in 1886
when their department was formed. Stephen Sales, former Troop Sergeant Major 7th Hussars,
their first chief inspector, helped initiate their high level of cavalry training.

Liverpool's chief constables had used mounted policemen — riding the Fire Brigade and prison van horses and often armed with cutlasses — from 1836 to 1886. In the latter year Chief Constable William Nott Bower formed the mounted police section. From this time forward, thoroughly trained mounted policemen and especially trained horses, were the basis of the department. They thus had an advantage over the former constables who were only temporarily chosen for mounted work with horses hired at random.

Though the size of the section necessarily diminished with the growth of the motor car, some twenty-nine constables, under an inspector and three sergeants, comprised this splendid body of the Force in 1966. These men were the recognised experts at handling large crowds and were an admired sight at the Grand National at Aintree race-course, the Liverpool show, the Liverpool and Everton football grounds and indeed whenever they supervised crowds on a grand occasion. Some idea of the value of this section is to be gained from the fact in the sixties the Watch Committee paid over £350 for each new horse they purchased for the section and a former Chief Constable, Joseph Smith, estimated that one police horse and rider did the equivalent work of twelve men in crowd control.

In spite of many heavy demands, on their professional expertise, however, daily patrols were performed throughout the City and displays of skill were given at a number of local shows. Members also competed, with distinction, in several national horse shows.

Liverpool Mounted Police Sergeant, c.1890
This police photograph is one of the earliest of a mounted officer in the Liverpool Force.
His small hat was similar to those worn by other Victorian era policemen when on routine duty with
ambulance or fire-engine horses. When a post became vacant in the 'mounties', however,
it was not unknown for circulars to be sent to United Kingdom cavalry regiments.

DOG SECTION

This section was another highly successful branch of the Force and one, like the mounted section, which was very popular with Liverpudlians. Police dogs were formally introduced, in 1954, into those divisions where an alarming number of attacks on women had been reported. They had an immediate effect and such attacks quickly declined. As a deterrent to violent crime and waves of hooliganism, the patrols of police handlers with their trained dogs had no equal. Many offenders ran away to avoid capture but were caught in pursuit by the dogs. This happened even though several of them deliberately ran towards busy thoroughfares to avoid capture by mingling with the crowds. The use of dogs also led to a marked increase in the arrest of the number of law-breakers hiding inside premises.

Thus, after a short time, the dog handlers and their charges became an accepted feature during the day in the business area of the City and were welcomed by the businessmen and the general public.

The police dog handlers were also asked to train dogs used by outside bodies in security work. They helped the Liverpool Airport Committee and the Denbighshire Constabulary, amongst others, in this way. Hence, by 1967, the Liverpool police dog handlers and their forty dogs fulfilled an integral role in City police work.

Police Dogs. During the early part of the twentieth century, several chief constables experimented with the use of dogs for tracking work and for dealing with thugs. This parade and inspection of dogs, probably Airedales, appears to be taking place near Stanley Railway Station, c.1910, which overlooked the Liverpool College and Police Athletic Ground, Prescot Road. This would indicate that Liverpool City Police Force was an early pioneer in the use of trained dogs.

EXPLOSIVES AND FIRE PREVENTION DEPARTMENT

This department, consisting of one inspector, one sergeant, and six constables was based at police headquaters in Hardman Street. It was responsible for the general safety of those warehouses registered under the Liverpool Corporation Act, 1921, and ensured that the many necessary anti-fire precautions were carried out.

The men's other duties were also very complex. They had to supervise the use of explosives in the City and on the Dock estate; examine the handling of dangerous cargoes, including petroleum and radioactive substances. They ensured that the dock buildings and ships were fumigated, and they enforced the provisions of the Explosives Act, Firearms Act and the Control of Explosives Order.

Their duties were seen as an extension of the work which had been undertaken by the Liverpool Police Fire Brigade from 1836 to 1941. This Brigade, in turn, had replaced the 'amateur' fire forces run by the town insurance companies.

At first, it was maintained by the Council as a 'stop-gap' force whilst they waited for an independent fire brigade to be established. Most of the firemen, were part-time —since their Main duties were concerned with police work. These 'fire-bobbies' operated manual engines, which were stored at their Temple Court headquarters, at the Prince's Dock, and in Lightbody Street and Prescot Street police stations. At the mercy of such crude equipment and using a woefully poor water supply for many years, the men were often unequal to the serious Liverpool dockland fires.

Fire-escape apparatus, 1883.
Two Police Firemen await inspection at the base of their 80 foot self-supporting fire-escape, 1883. The fire crew have removed the small wheeled 'front dolly', shown to the right of the picture. When the large-wheeled ladder escape was attached in a horizontal position to the dolly the completed unit was drawn by horses as a conventional 4 wheeled cart.

The Police Fire Brigade on Parade. The meticulous care lavished on both the Constable's uniform and fire brigade equipment are obvious in this official police photograph. The lamps, harness and fire brigade helmet are particularly striking at this parade and inspection, c.1890. Such events usually occurred at the Central Fire Station when it was not unknown for the steam fire engines to be florally decorated to mark the occasion.

Conditions did improve, however, as the fire insurance companies agreed to pay their share of the cost of running the Brigade and as better equipment — including the horse-drawn steam pumping engines of the eighteen seventies — and more police fire stations were added. Between 1851 and 1861, for example, the firemen increased from 72 to 149, and the stations from 7 to 17.

This remarkable police photograph captures a splendid team of four horses harnessed to the Hornby steam fire-engine, in 1898. They are driven past admiring crowds in Lime Street, opposite St. George's Hall. The police officers include two firemen wearing their gleaming German silver helmets and the specially trained team-master with reins and horsewhip to hand.

By the end of the century, the Brigade had undergone an amazing transformation. The growth of the use of the telephone, first used by the Brigade in 1881, was a typical symbol of this change. By 1897, petroleum-powered fire engines were beginning to replace the steam engines and a fine new central fire station was opened at Hatton Garden, 24th October, 1899. Thus, the City entered the twentieth century with a highly efficient force and it remained so until the formation of the National Fire Service.

The Explosives and Fire Prevention Department maintained these high standards and their services were in constant demand, especially following the new scientific developments after the Second World War. This was especially the case with the expansion of the Dingle Oil Installation and with the development of the Linacre Gas Works. At the latter, coal was converted to a petroleum distillate for the production of a low toxic gas.

'Siemens' Police and Fire Signals Box, 1897-1929. A Police Sergeant, 31A, with Liver Bird insignia and traditional 'stick' clearly in view, supervises the use by his colleague of the open signalsbox, c.1892.

Liverpool's motorised firemen, 1901.
This petroleum-fuelled fire engine was reputed to be the first of its type in Britain. The fine body of men shown are under the supervision of the Deputy Superintendent of the Brigade, Chief Inspector Thomas. The Daimler motor chemical vehicle was fitted with a body constructed at the Royal Coachworks, Hope Street, Liverpool. Clearly visible is the 'alarm gong' first used in Liverpool in 1898 to replace the less effective whistle warnings.

At the docks, the constables supervised those vessels loading and discharging radioactive material. Irradiated full elements were increasingly brought, during the 1960's, into the country via Liverpool for processing. These consignments demanded special interest but the United Kingdom Atomic Energy Authority were thankful that under the eye of the Department they became regarded as routine.

THE SPECIAL CONSTABULARY CORPS

In contrast to the bullying reputation of the earliest Liverpool 'specials' in the 1830's and the 1840's, the members of the Special Constabulary Corps had established a distinguished reputation for themselves by the close of the Liverpool City Force.

At the stormy Parliamentary elections in the nineteenth century the specials had to be recruited to supplement the regular policemen who were often unable, by themselves, to control immense unruly mobs which traditionally gathered on such occasions. The Victorian specials' brutish attitude to the volatile members of the public often inflamed a threatening riotous situation, as was shown in the election on 3rd July 1841.

Not all such temporary constables came from the ranks of the badly-behaved, poorer classes of Liverpudlians. Among the most famous of their voluntary members was the noveliest Charles Dickens. He relished his 'slumming expeditions', with regular policemen to protect him, whether in Liverpool, London or New York. Whenever he visited Liverpool, he apparently enjoyed roaming about the docklands to see how the hosts of sailors behaved whilst ashore.

In 'The Uncommercial Traveller', he described his walking tours as he ventured into the haunts of the port's landsharks. Partly for his own safety, he enrolled as a 'special' constable, had his identity photograph taken, went 'on parade' and, in the company of experienced policemen, went to see the 'various unlawful traps' which were 'set every night for Jack'. In Dickens' opinion, at the time of his description, about 1860, the general body of Liverpool policemen conducted themselves as 'an admirable force' and he wrote that the constabulary 'tempers its remarkable vigilance with still more remarkable discretion'. -

Many other civic-spirited members of the public, in time, also echoed his admiration. At the close of the Liverpool Police Force the tradition had long-been established that only those citizens were selected for 'special' duty who were able to prove that they had a high regard for constabulary responsibilities. In 1967 about 397 men and women 'specials' assisted the regular police officers during the course of the year. They became especially valued during the manpower crisis of this period. In particular they undertook duties at a seemingly ever-increasing round of major events in the city, including the Liverpool Show, the Woolton Show and Liverpool Parks fire-works displays.

CADET CORPS

This valuable section of the Force — the first of its type in the country — was established by Chief Constable Charles Martin in 1949 and grew prodigiously after that year. As a means of recruiting prospective consables, the Corps was first class. The successful candidates were given an early experience of modern police work and whilst so doing were given the opportunity to improve their educational background and develop their own hobbies and interests.

By the 'Sixties, therefore, members of the authorised 150 strong section, attended 'Outward Bound' courses at Aberdovey Sea School, Ullswater and Eskdale, and many took part in the Duke of Edinburgh's Award Scheme. Members of the corps also attended Childwall Hall County College and Millbank Commercial College to broaden their education.

PLANNING SECTION

The Planning Section — like the Warrant Section of the Force — was a modern department, undertaking highly specialised administrative work. Its members became responsible for preparing graphic and accurate plans in support of various prosecutions, including those for murder, manslaughter, larceny, 'breaking' offences, gross indecency, rape, armed robbery and drunken driving.

They also prepared plans relating to fatal and other serious traffic accidents, and assisted the C.I.D. with 'scene of the crime' plans, area maps and display posters. From time to time, too, they also organised crime-prevention exhibitions and recruiting campaigns. This section, therefore, did much to foster police-public relationship.

RECREATION

Chief Constable Nott Bower helped to form the Police Athletic Club to foster the outdoor recreational pursuits of his young constables.

By the 1960's the recreational facilities, both indoor and outdoor, had expanded immensely. There were some seventeen active sections in the Liverpool Police Recreational Society — Athletics, Angling, Basketball, Bowls, Chess, Cricket, Concert Party and Drama Group, Darts, Football, Golf, Horticulture, Shooting, Snooker, Swimming, Table Tennis and Tug-of-War.

Functions, such as dances, suppers, socials and hot-pots, were regularly held at the Fairfield Clubhouse. Other functions, arranged in the divisions by their own social and welfare committees, along with those sponsored by the Athletic Society and the Comrades' Association, ensured a full and varied programme each year.

THE POLICE BAND

The Police Band, 1897.
This was formed originally in 1865 to provide a source of recreation for its members and to entertain the public. Its members, shown here awaiting inspection, played free of charge in some of Liverpool's famous parks. Whenever possible, too, they performed on St. George's Plateau. A talented group of officers later formed the Liverpool City Police Minstrel orchestra and Variety Group, and met with significant success.

When the Liverpool Police Force was amalgamated with Bootle Police Force, in 1967, the Liverpool Police Band had been in existence for almost one hundred years. The original members, with the help of Chief Constable Major John Greig, came together partly because they wanted to provide a healthy source of recreation — which were few at the time — for the Liverpool poor. Their main aim was to entertain and win the respect of these poorer classes of Liverpool folk.

For many years, therefore, the constables made it their business to play, free of charge, each summer Saturday evening in one of the large Liverpool Parks. They tried to spur other Liverpool bands into doing likewise but their efforts, at first, met with little success. Whenever possible, too, they played at the Penny Concerts for the poor at St. George's Hall.

Though weakened from time to time by a shortage of members, the voluntary group established and maintained very high musical standards. Not surprisingly, too, the men were also asked to perform on many civic occasions.

During 1966, itself, they carried out 111 engagements and, notably, at the request of the B.B.C. attended for a recording of a programme commemorating the life of composer Vaughan Williams. Having, on several occasions, previously broadcast their performances for the B.B.C., they rose to the occasion with distinction. In the same year, they also assisted the Royal Liverpool Philharmonic Orchestra when it sought a large number of instrumentalists.

POLICE STATIONS

Though there were some notable exceptions, many of the Liverpool police stations — or 'bridewells' as they were originally termed — were by the 1960's terribly out of date.

The stations themselves provided little actual service to the community, they were expensive to staff, equip and maintain. Originally, they had provided a great service as a place to keep the violent and the drunken prisoners of the City whilst they awaited trial. The stations had also on occasions protected the police from threatening mob elements in the port.

In 1836 there were only two bridewells in the Town, namely those at Rose Hill and Seel Street. All the better-constructed stations, for many years after this time, were at the docks. Six years later, the main bridewell at Exchange Street West, and three smaller stations, in Vauxhall Road, Brick Street and Hotham Street, were added to the total number of town stations. By 1852 another four had been built at Athol Street, Prescot Street, Essex Street and Olive Street — all built to absorb the criminal element in the growing population living between the parish and borough boundaries.

These, and several of the later stations, were constructed in a fortified style in the heart of

Athol Street Bridewell.
One of four built in a fortified style, c.1852. The others were in Prescot Street, Essex Street
and Olive Street. These 'new' police stations were particularly needed after the influx, in the 1840's,
of a flood of immigrants into Liverpool. It was the practice for crowds to gather outside some of them
to hear if their associates had been detained on charges by the police. The high
defensive perimeter walls were to discourage any unlawful attempts
to secure a prisoner's release.

the roughest and most heavily populated districts of the town. The Derby Road Bridewell, for example, was erected in 1867 for "a numerous and rough population".

Many of these older stations had their own characteristic type of prisoner. Prescot Street Bridewell, for example, was infamous for drunken carters; Vauxhall road Bridewell was deluged by drunken assailants; and Hotham Street, in the heart of the town, was renowned for its "gay young ladies and fast young men, of a superior class". Huge crowds, too, particularly in the rougher districts, gathered at night outside the bridewells to see if charges were to be brought against their associates.

As social conditions improved, however, such scenes became infrequent. With the expansion of the City and the consequent reorganisation of the Force into more and more police divisions, the old stations became badly situated for the needs of the modern police constables.

Thus, by the 1960's, though the Borough Force possessed some of the most modern computer technology and communications the constables were greatly handicapped by antiquated stations often in out-of-the-way places. These fitted badly into the changing pattern of City policing.

Part Four

CHIEF CONSTABLES
OF LIVERPOOL
1836-1967

MICHAEL WHITTY, 1836-44

With many citizens apparently reluctant to support the introduction of the police, in 1836 — as others were too, in other large cities — Head Constable Michael Whitty faced the most difficult task that any principal officer of the seaport had to come to terms with.

He had, no experience to guide him, met serious difficulty in obtaining suitable officers and recruits, and he had none of the records or appliances at his disposal which are regarded as commonplace in 'modern' police forces. It says much for him, and for his men, that he did succeed in gradually overcoming all these difficulties.

His strong sense of discipline probably resulted from his early Catholic education. After attending St. Peter's College, Wexford, he went to Maynooth to study for the Roman Catholic priesthood. He travelled widely, went to Dublin, then London. There taking the post of editor of the 'Journal' he continued in that position until 1833 when he became Superintendent of the Night Watch.

Impulsive, but of a kind nature, he had a tenacious memory and it was said he could call every man in the Force by his name and rank. He set out to discipline his new charges with untiring zeal. He was probably prompted in no small way by an attack on his life in July 1835. Going to the rescue of watchmen trapped by a ferocious mob in the Vauxhall Road Bridewell, he was himself attacked. Had not two young bystanders assisted him through the bridewell doorway — smashed open by the axes and staves of the mob — he might have been killed. For a long time after, he had 200 cutlasses stored for his men at the main bridewell.

Under Whitty, the professional standards steadily improved. His ideas for policing the town and docks, for increasing the efficiency of the fire police and safeguarding the health of his men were refreshingly progressive in a period of dire economic and political unrest.

At this time it was not unusual for frustrated people in the town to express their dissatisfaction violently at municipal elections. When he came to office, 20,000 lived in cellars that were worse than pigsties and another 40,000 lived in the narrow courts where conditions were appalling.

Continually short of qualified manpower, he had to build up the morale of the Force working under very poor conditions. Badly paid, on call at any time — working in darkness and inclement weather — his men had to reside where they were ordered to do so. Some of the Orange-Catholic antagonisms even penetrated his Force. He must have been disappointed, but hardly surprised, to find that out of the 360 men recruited in 1860, only 172 were still in the Force two years later. This was similar to the experiences of other large cities in this period.

Naturally, though he was continually praised by the Watch Committee, he did not escape public censure. He was particularly opposed by the licensed publicans who resented his 'spies', or plain clothes detectives, checking their premises. Nevertheless, he left the Force after eleven years' service having soundly established it on a firm basis.

After his resignation, the Watch Committee paid him a great tribute, recording that "in the performance of the arduous duties attached to his office, the zeal, energy and ability, displayed by him, were not more conspicuous than his uniform discretion and judgement, combining in a peculiar degree decision of conduct with the utmost courtesy and forebearance."

When Whitty resigned from office he again turned to journalism, founding and editing the 'Liverpool Post'. His fearless, forthright condemnation of whatever he believed to be wrong made him one of the most widely read journalists on Merseyside.

He conflicted with Bishop Goss, over a reference in a pastoral letter to the reporting of the scandals of the day in the 'penny paper daily'; he attacked the bishop's views on the temporal power of the Pope. Father Nugent was also criticized in the editorial columns for buying and printing The Northern Press, and there is no doubt that Whitty was a source of embarrassment to the Catholic leaders in the City.

On the other hand, he alone defended the Bishop in his attitude to the sending of children to Reform Schools, since he favoured the schools himself and it was Whitty's violent editorial campaign against the City Council that caused the Home Secretary to override the Council's decision and appoint Father Nugent as the first paid Catholic Chaplain to Walton Gaol.

When, in 1851, a County Court Judge made some scathing criticism of Liverpool people, a Liverpool Post placard bearing words which the judge took as offensive was placed in the precincts of the court. The judge ordered Whitty's arrest. Whitty's admirers punctuated the subsequent proceedings with cheers and jeers and the judge called on the bailiffs to arrest the offenders. The bailiffs replied that they could not arrest the entire Court, whereon the Judge fined them each five pounds for incompetence.

On being fined, Whitty refused to pay and was sent to Lancaster Gaol for seven days. Over two thousand signatures of notable people of all denominations were affixed to a petition for the removal of the Judge. Whitty's fine, and that of the bailiffs was paid and he was immediately released. After a hearing of nine days, Judge Ramshay was dismissed and eventually found himself faced with eighteen hundred pounds legal costs.

Whitty continued to write until his sudden death on 10th June, 1873. He was buried in Anfield Cemetery, the service being read by one of his former opponents, Father Guy, O.S.H. The large crowd of mourners was a solid tribute to this fearless man whose forthrightness won him the affection of many friends and the respect of his adversaries.

HENRY MILLER, 1844

As soon as Whitty resigned, the Watch Committee widely advertised for a successor. They eventually appointed Henry Miller. Having been in the Glasgow police force for eight years, he came with an excellent service record and the 'Liverpool Courier' reported, on 28th February, that during his service in Glasgow he had repeatedly shown sound judgement and was firm and determined. He also possessed a broad knowledge of criminal law.

His stay of eight months in the Liverpool office, however, was by far the shortest of any Chief Constable in the history of the Force. Appointed on 27th February, 1844, he resigned on 26th October in the same year. Authoritarian in his attitude towards his men, he departed completely from Whitty's humane ideals. On 1st June, for example, he asked the Watch Committee to appoint a competent person to the new office of drill-master. He thus planned to introduce greater military discipline and rigidity.

By 5th October, the Watch Committee felt that something was amiss, and they appointed a sub-committee to inquire into the state of the police force. Before this committee reported, another sub-committee — the daily board of the Watch Committee accused Miller of flagrantly disobeying the Watch Committee. The sub-committee's findings, too, cast a shadow on Miller's reputation.

They agreed, after a thorough cross-examination of Whitty, Miller, the Commissioners of the Police, the Superintendents and Inspectors, that the printed regulations of the Force had not been correctly carried out since Miller commenced his duties. He had failed to visit the different stations and patrol the town at irregular hours during the day and night. In the short period since Miller's appointment, moreover, the Force had declined in efficiency, because he had chosen "young and inexperienced" police inspectors. The Committee also felt he had been too aloof from his men and had been so haughty and overbearing with his senior officers that he had lost their confidence. Finally, he had introduced a harsh system of drill and marched prisoners on foot through the town chained by ankle fetters to each other.

This state of affairs came to a head when he flagrantly flouted the authority of the Watch Committee after the Birkenhead Watch Commissioners asked for his services and the help of fifty of his men. His request to the committee was denied because they felt he was required to keep order "amidst the immense concourse of persons" assembling at the pierheads for disembarkations from the steamboats.

In the very face of this refusal, Miller crossed the Mersey at seven one morning and did not return to Liverpool until three in the afternoon. Not only did he set a terrible example of insubordination, said the Watch Committee, but — because the chief town fire officers accompanied him — he left the port without a man competent to deal with a serious fire.

The Watch Committee gave him the chance to resign and he accepted it. The 'Liverpool Mercury' took his side, believing that the Watch Committee seriously weakened his power and had not given him sufficient scope to use his own discretion. Thus the newspaper touched on the question of who had the ultimate right to control the Borough Force — the Watch Committee or the Chief Constable.

The Municipal Corporations Act, 1835, was surprisingly silent about the issue. Liverpool's Watch Committee had taken their power from the section of the Act empowering them to make regulations "for preventing neglect or abuse, and rendering constables efficient in the discharge of their duties", and had accepted the provision to dismiss any constable "whom they shall think negligent in the discharge of his duty". This remained an unresolved question until the earlier legislation was replaced by the Police Act, 1964, for it was never tested in the courts of law.

MATTHEW DOWLING, 1845-52

Matthew Maurice George Dowling officiated during the critical period of rapid town growth and dock expansion. On the one hand, he faced an alarming increase in the town's population with the sudden unprecedented influx of Irish immigrants. On the other hand, there was a great increase in property with the building of new docks, warehouses and dwellinghouses. This forced him to continually re-organise his command. Faced by the discomfort of extra duties, particularly those involving the diseased and crime-ridden Irish ghettos, many constables quit the Force. Others were dismissed for drunkenness.

Fortunately, he was an experienced man, being a barrister at law and a Commissioner of the Liverpool force at the time of Miller's resignation. An able police officer, he had moved from the London Metropolitan Force to Liverpool.

Though the facilities for drunkenness and prostitution taxed both Dowling and his men to the to the full they had to meet an even greater menace in 1845. Swamping the port and stretching the manpower of the Borough Force to breaking point, came the tidal wave of immigrants attempting to escape the consequences of the Irish potato famine. From 1st January until the end of June 1847, some 30,000 Irish landed. Of these, 60,000 to 80,000 located themselves in the already overcrowded lodginghouses and in the town cellars. Dr. Duncan, the town's first Medical Officer of Health, found that the whole of the parish cellar population — upwards of 20,000 persons — were without any type of toilets. Some twenty-six streets between Scotland Road and Vauxhall Road, containing about 1,200 front houses, had some two-thirds of their number without either yard, privy or ash-pit.

In Liverpool, therefore, in the late 'forties, there existed many of the conditions which fostered law-breaking on a large scale. Dowling showed in the Police Statistical Returns for 1847, that the great increase in crime was largely caused by the immigrants. Daily fights and brawls became common in the Irish communities.

He had to be particularly suspicious of any political movement at this period. Thus, he had to prepare for the threatened Chartist demonstrations in 1848. His men were sent to keep watch on the infamous lodging-houses which were the homes of habitual thieves and vagabonds. They were instructed to report the re-opening of cellars, and prepare returns showing the number of courts on their beats. During the 1849 cholera epidemic, the men gave Dr. Duncan every assistance too, Three sergeants were appointed in the same year to disinfect the various lodging-houses.

On March 17th, St. Patrick's Day and 12th July, the Anniversary of the Battle of the Boyne, Dowling had to prepare for the most serious Catholic — Orange demonstrations. St. Patrick's Day, 1848, saw him feverishly organising his men.

At seven o'clock in the morning the mayor and the magistrates met in the Sessions House, where all the 'specials' waited — filling the two courts, the grand jury room, the lobbies and all the cellars. Every special captain marshalled his own men and supplied each with a truncheon. Charles Turner was appointed commander-in-chief of the reserves and Michael Whitty, the former chief constable, his lieutenant.

Meanwhile, Dowling mustered the regular police at the different bridewells. A troop of the 11th Hussars was at Lucas's Repository, the 52nd Regiment, sent from Preston, was stationed at the North Corporation School and companies of the 60th Rifles were distributed at different posts in the town. Members of the Lancashire police force mustered at the main bridewell and Borough Gaol. Fortunately, with the would-be trouble makers aware of the preparations, St. Patrick's Day passed peacefully.

With this and similar situations to deal with, Dowling constantly reformed his Force to meet the new threats. Notably, he appointed the Force's first chief detective. By January, 1846, he had eleven men acting as detectives, collectively receiving £2.15.0d. per month for wearing their own clothing whilst on duty.

Working conditions for his men were harsh and remuneration was poor. In 1845, some of them received their first pay rise since 1836 — two whole shillings a week! During 1846, 168 constables were reported for drunkenness. Needless to say it was the temptations put before the constables and not the pay rise which lay at the root of this problem.

In addition, the huge crowds visiting the town after 1844, due to the cheaper railway fares, caused his men extra work, as did the fact they had to watch the extra 3,460 houses and 44 warehouses constructed in the Borough in 1846. Finding no ready solution to this ever increasing work-load for his men and threatened by dire shortage of manpower, he travelled in November 1847 to Manchester and Birmingham in search of fresh ideas.

He was eventually allowed to incorporate some of the Mancunian innovations into the Liverpool Force. Included was greater freedom for the Chief Constable. He introduced the much needed rank of sergeant to the force. He tried to obtain more comfortable living quarters for many of his men. Nevertheless, the town environment made the life of each constable one of constant turmoil — each undertaking an average of 10½ hours duty each day, exclusive of his attendance at court, at drills and to collect his pay.

Liverpool's magistrates paid tribute to him for his sterling work. Yet they dismissed him in March 1852 for attempting to preserve his unblemished record by removing from the North Division Police Book, a report by Sergeant Tomlinson which impugned the conduct of the police. Superintendent Towerson was also dismissed for making a false report. Dowling's record in very difficult circumstances was a good one, this aberration apart.

JOHN GREIG, 1852-1881

Captain John James Greig was a very able and intelligent officer and was of the same fine mould as the town's first Chief Constable, M.J. Whitty. Faced by the perennial problems of excessive town violence, political unrest and shortage of manpower, his task was made no easier by the constant opposition of the Liberal-supported Vigilance Committee.

The son of an officer who had served in the East India Company, he was born in September 1807 in Edinburgh, where he also received his education. After leaving school, he became for two years, a midshipman in the service of the East India Company, but in 1828 he obtained a commission in the 24th Queen's Regiment. He was engaged on recruiting service in Glasgow for two and a half years. In 1842 he was appointed Staff Officer of Pensions at Manchester, but remained there only six months, being transferred to the Liverpool district until 1852.

He personal attributes were of the highest order and though some alleged he was too dignified and too reserved, this was merely his military instincts which insisted he hold some 'distance' from those beneath him. His detachment, therefore, was simply 'official' and confined to the parade. In truth, none could be more genial in heart or manner.

He was, in fact, very personal in his approach and he regularly visited those in police custody, at the main police-station on Sunday afternoons. Sometimes, he would go there with a clergy-man and give the inmates a few kindly words of admonition. On other occasions, he would scold those brought in for drunkenness and violence who appeared dirty and unshaven on 'the clean shirt day', or sabbath.

Greig was something of a social reformer, too, for he stressed, in 1857, the urgent need for more places of recreation in Liverpool. Compared to other large British towns, he felt Liverpool had few parks and pleasure grounds within reach of many of those living in the overcrowded quarters of the Borough.

He also had to face the growing threat of organised strikes. He and his men coped well with several potentially dangerous strikes, but in February 1879, the dock labourers struck and the local militia had to be called in.

His work was made no easier by the Irish immigrants — an aggregate of one million of them landing in Liverpool between 1849 and 1853. Such people were only too ready to join any impulsive demonstrations of protest such as the Liverpool bread riots in 1850 during his predecessor's incumbency.

The Irish however, developed their most menacing form as Fenian supporters. Greig's prudent action in speedily dispatching information which came to his notice, in February 1867, prevented serious Fenian outrages in both Chester and Dublin. When asked by the Chief Constable of Salford to assist, with 100 Liverpool men, in keeping the peace at the execution of the Fenian prisoners, or 'Manchester Martyrs', in November of the same year, he refused, because he had sufficient to do in watching the Liverpool-based supporters. As we have seen, they nearly succeeded, in 1881, in destroying the Liverpool Town Hall and the police residence at Hatton Garden.

Meanwhile, he and his men had to keep a watch on the lower classes, who indulged in violence at town elections. His men also witnessed serious outrages at the Anfield foot races, in 1856, and the dangerous snowball riots in Exchange High Street and Exchange Street West in 1854, 1855 and 1865 which required 60, 100 and over 200 policemen respectively, to restore order.

Obviously, the physical expansion of the town at the same time continued to burden the Force. Between 1st January 1857 and 1st October 1859, some 4,737 houses and numerous warehouses, factories and stables were built in the borough, and the population increased by 30,000, yet Greig was only granted an extra twenty constables to cope with the expansion. It was not surprising, therefore, that he had to resist a proposal to reduce the military cavalry force, of 110 men, and an infantry force of 136, quartered at Liverpool's North Fort.

His was also a constant battle to attract new recruits. Each constable received three days' annual leave of absence with pay, had no weekday holiday and was only granted leave of absence every sixteenth day. However, Liverpool was not alone in this Hull, Bristol Bradford, London, Manchester, Leicester, Birmingham, Edinburgh, Glasgow and Leeds, had similar problems.

Several of Greig's reforms were noteworthy. By the end of his period of office, the detective department — previously a somewhat independent branch of the force — was a fully integrated unit. Liverpool's position as a great seaport would have afforded the means of escape for notorious criminals if this department had not willingly co-operated with other police forces. Each detective was selected for his 'sharpness' and his duties, as member of a small section of sixteen men, often took him beyond Liverpool. In the winter months of 1867, for example, they traced cotton valued at over £2,000 — stolen from Liverpool warehouses — to Birmingham, Sheffield and other large towns. The department also tracked down grain thieves and a gang which systematically scuttled ships. Their work involving the Fenians, too, was first rate.

Greig's sympathy for the humbler town people, as we have seen, was sincere. The police band was formed about this time, to entertain them. Greig's men also distributed aid to the poor and needy. During the severe frost in the early Winter of 1861, for example, under the patronage of the mayor they helped those on their beats they knew to be deserving of relief. This helped prevent large unruly crowds from assembling in the streets. Altogether, they issued some 9,000 bread tickets, 6,720 soup tickets, 275 coal tickets and 50 rugs.

This was a period when the men had to safeguard many public functions. Several fine public buildings were completed — including the William Brown Library, the Museum, the Walker Art Gallery and St. George's Hall — and the police were required to assist at the opening ceremonies. A succession of royal visits and requests for help from many other towns and places overseas, placed further demands on Greig and his men.

He held the head constableship, with rare distinction, for some twenty years, and felt it his duty to resign, as he said, because he did not have "the activity of former years". On 30th August 1881, the Watch Committee were fortunate to have John W. Nott Bower succeed him, a man who was also to rank as one of Liverpool's finest Chief Constables.

JOHN NOTT BOWER, 1881-1902

Captain John William Nott Bower was a worthy successor to Captain Greig. His fresh outlook and his programme of reform came when it was most needed. Born in York on 20th March, 1849, he was the son of a barrister-at-law. When only 16 years of age, he passed the entrance examination to the Royal Military College at Sandhurst. He apparently saw little opportunity in the Army, however, and decided to take up a police career.

He was fortunate in that W.E. Forster who was his father's friend, was able, in 1872, to give him a letter of introduction to Lord Hartingdon, then Chief Secretary for Ireland. In January 1873, he entered the Constabulary Depot in Phoenix Park, Dublin, beginning a police career that was to last fifty-two years.

In the latter part of 1876, after working in Limerick, he returned to Dublin to take command of No.1 12 (Ulster) Company, at the Constabulary Depot in Phoenix Park. In 1878, he accepted the appointment of Chief Constable of Leeds.

His stay there was short and during 1881 he applied and was selected for the vacant Liverpool Head Constableship — an office he was to hold for twenty-one years.

He knew when he accepted office that the port was infamous for violence. For several years at the beginning of his Liverpool service the reported cases of serious wounding, stabbing and other assaults, averaged 250 each year, whilst the number of cases of common assault amounted to 2,000

According to Nott Bower, there were streets in the Scotland Road Division which were unsafe for respectable persons to enter and where even the police could not patrol alone. In such an area, too, petty larcenies due to extreme pressures of want, were high. As we have seen, too, the High Rip Gang rumours did little to help the police in their work.

Many absolute ruffians lived in the town, who were responsible for frequent scenes of turbulence in the City. Amongst these and other nuisances, the constables had to supervise the female fish-sellers in Great Charlotte Street opposite the Town fish Market, check people wandering the streets at night without shelter, supervise assemblies of people in Church Street on festive occasions, keep a close watch on street-betting and the widespread use of foul language. Finally, they had to deal with the alarming Liverpool Dock Strike, in 1890. This unrest constantly forced Nott Bower to attempt to invoke new ideas. Though he found it a slow and arduous process, he eventually reformed the two cumbersome police divisions reorganising them into five smaller ones. To offset the pressure of population growth on the Force, he helped initiate the formation of the mounted police section in 1886. He also induced the Watch Committee to purchase three patrol wagons — the forerunners of the police motor cars — in 1891. In this he followed the example of the principal towns of the U.S.A. and helped link the wagons and bridewells by the use of the many private telephones which were made available to the Force.

These wagons were horse-drawn 'long cars', which held four men on each side of the car; at their centre there was a removable stretcher for carrying violent and disorderly prisoners. Generally, they each carried three constables, but in times of special need, the wagons were capable of accommodating an entire section of one sergeant and his nine constables. Thus

Nott Bower aimed by their adoption to quell speedily the noisy and dangerous brawls characteristic of the City. He also felt they saved the citizens the vulgarity of having to witness violent prisoners dragged by the police through the public thoroughfares.

His mobilisation of the Force had been prompted by his successful initiation of the Police Ambulance System. When he first came to office, he was appalled by the callousness shown in the removal of persons who had met with accidents, or had taken ill in the streets. A stretcher, with ignorant and uninstructed bearers was the only method used for the removal of the injured. In collaboration with Reginald Harrison, barrister-at-law, he drew up plans for an improved system.

At their instigation, in May 1882, the Watch Committee agreed to supply eighteen of the police and fire stations in the city with a small wheeled litter, or ambulance; these were a great improvement on the old stretchers because they required only two men to work them and not four. At this time, nineteen hand ambulances were also used in the City so that every part of Liverpool had this humane means of conveyance for the injured.

Gradually, the litters were replaced by the horse-drawn ambulances. This type of ambulance, which had been in use in the U.S.A. for some time, was worked in conjunction with a telegraph system and ensured that a medical officer and appliances were prompt in arriving at the scene of the accident. By 1884, the Watch Committee had a horse ambulance stationed at the Northern Hospital and within nine months of its establishment it had conveyed some 272 cases. Later, ambulances were stationed at the Royal Infirmary, the Royal Southern Hospital, the Northern Hospital and the Stanley Hospital.

Liverpool City Police Ambulance.
This horse-drawn ambulance, 1886, was modelled on those in use in the United States of America.
The vehicle, in readiness in the yard of the Central Fire Station, clearly shows its Liverbird insignia beneath
its nearside nightlamp. Such a vehicle was a vast improvement upon the earlier stretchers
and small-wheeled litters, or 'handcarts'.

A further 'humane' problem the Head Constable had to cope with was that of 'wandering lunatics'. The lunatics were not law-breakers, but simply persons of unsound mind found wandering by the police. Until 1893, they were sent to the Mill Road Infirmary and admitted at the request of the police. About this time the assistant medical officer refused to accept any such persons from the police. He would accept only those persons who had been certified as proper cases for asylum treatment, and who had been removed to the Asylum by a Magistrate's Order. For the remainder of Nott Bower's term of office, the police had to face this problem, and as late as November 1899, he related how some of his constables had been forced to wander back and forth between their bridewell and several workhouses until one of them took the lunatic in.

All these problems came on top of his need to re-organise his men when the City boundaries were extended in 1895. They had to patrol within an area which increased from 6,524 acres to 15,252, to safeguard 399 miles of streets, where formerly they had watched 277 miles. At the same time, the population increased from 503,967 to 642,095, and the rateable value from £3,203,000 to £3,787,226. To meet these new demands his force expanded from 1,294 men to 1,460.

In the main, these men remained a loyal and efficient crime preventative body. As a measure of his appreciation, Nott Bower helped foster the founding of the Liverpool Police Athletic Club.

Nevertheless, his men did come in for severe criticism with the mismanagement, in 1888,

In November 1856, H.M.I. of police inspected the Liverpool force for the first time. He recorded "they were a very fine body of men". Sefton Park became a popular midday venue for the men to assemble for this annual parade, as shown, c.1898, at the review field.

of the general store in the Hatton Garden police section house. Wild and inaccurate newspaper reports condemned the store as a 'Police Boozing Den'. After the strictest investigations, however, it was found that some non-members of the Force and non-resident constables had been supplied with beer at the store, but there was no evidence of excessive drinking or disorderly conduct.

In spite of this slur, there can be no doubt that Nott Bower had an efficient and praiseworthy Force. The men distinguished themselves on numerous occasions, and, notably during the visit of Queen Victoria, from 11th to 13th May 1886, when she stayed as a guest of the Corporation and opened the Liverpool Exhibition that year.

Their record of duty was quite remarkable because on 11th, their first parade was at 6 o'clock in the morning and from that time until 1 a.m. on 12th (nineteen hours) the men were on continuous duty in the streets without even an interval for refreshments (which they had to bring in their pockets and eat, as opportunity offered, in the streets). Again, they paraded, at 8.30 a.m. on the 12th and remained on duty until 1 a.m. on 13th (sixteen and a half hours) under similar circumstances. They had to be out at 7.30 a.m. on 14th so that they actually performed the equivalent of four and a half days work in two days. Much of the duty was undertaken, too, in very inclement weather. Their admiration for the Queen, moreover, was fully shown on the 13th, when at their request, as the Queen drove to the Exhibition, the men were allowed to remove their helmets, and join in the cheers of the crowd as Her Majesty passed by.

Many requests for assistance from parties outside the Borough were received and granted, Nott Bower, was even asked for advice from as far afield as Budapest, Hong Kong, and Southern Africa. His unique ability and experience, however, inevitably drew him to London, and on 21st March 1902 he was elected to the Commissionership of Police of the City of London.

Pictured right, Constable Collins.
Liverpool City Constabulary was highly regarded for the general efficiency and the smart appearance of its policemen. Constable Collins, in traffic duty stance, was a model of how the men were expected to appear at important public events. His uniform, c.1890, strikingly includes his 'on duty' armlet, his whistle chain, his metallic belt plate* and his parade gloves. The chevron on his right arm would indicate that he is still a constable 'second class'. From 1865; first class constables wore two chevrons.

* *First introduced in 1853 to replace belt buckles.*

LEONARD DUNNING, 1902-11

Sir Leonard Dunning was born in London in June 1860 and was educated at Eton and Exeter College, Oxford, where he gained a degree in jurisprudence. When twenty-two years of age he joined the Royal Irish constabulary and served until 1895 as a district inspector. He left this post to become the assistant chief constable of Liverpool under Nott Bower.

His official connection with Liverpool lasted seventeen years, for he became head constable in 1902. His period of service as Chief of the Liverpool Force covered some of the stormiest episodes in the history of the Town. One of these was connected with the sectarian strife which had disgraced Liverpool for many years and reached a high-water mark in the Summer of 1909.

Orange stalwarts were incensed as detailed below, and attacked a Roman Catholic street procession in the North end of the City; rioting on a serious scale ensued, and the mounted police were compelled to charge the mobs. Many people were injured and there were numerous arrests.

The outcome was a Government inquiry. This appeased the ultra Protestant section, which, under the leadership of the prominent Dr. George Wise, had demanded it. A.J. Ashton, K.C. sat as the Home Office Commissioner at the inquiry, which lasted for twenty-four days, in February 1910. He investigated, amongst others, charges brought against the Chief Constable and his officers. it was to the credit of the Force, that both Dunning and his men were completely exonerated.

During the inquiry, the Commissioner suggested that a board of conciliation should be formed. This proposal was later acted upon and a committee, under the presidency of Lord Derby, was established to facilitate greater understanding between the denominations. Ensuing conferences helped to relieve the tension in the various communities and to begin the long process of establishing religious tolerance between them.

Following quickly on the heels of this upheaval came the great labour unrest, in 1911, in Liverpool. The Summer that year was marked by a series of transport strikes. Firstly, in June, the seamen struck and they were followed by the dockers. Both stoppages initiated a wave of enthusiasm for trade unions. In August, the railway goods porters followed the stevedores by striking for better wages and a shorter working week. At Great Howard Street Goods Station, the porters came out on 5th August, followed by those at the Waterloo Dock and Edge Hill. Soon, the entire docks were at a standstill and the stoppages spread to other railway centres. The police thereon had to be called in to provide escorts for food lorries leaving the passenger stations, through which the food was being transported. There were no violent outrages, it would appear, until the police contingents from Leeds and Birmingham were called in, followed by troops who eventually numbered 5,000. The violence reached a head on the afternoon on Sunday 13th August, or Bloody Sunday as it was more commonly known. The hot summer weather brought people outdoors and disturbances occurred.

Foodstuffs taken by carts received police, military and magistrates' escorts and, together with the crowds observing these unusual processions, some 90,000 congregated on St. George's Plateau to hear the leaders of the Labour Movement address them there. The

'Bloody Sunday', 13th August, 1911. The Riot Act was read twice, outside St. Georges Hall and in Christian Street.

meeting was broken up. Some suggested that policemen had sparked the unrest by cudgelling onlookers at windowsills. Others blamed the overturning of a cart driven by an alleged blackleg. In the ensuing mayhem some two hundred people including 'many innocent persons' received injuries.

The Riot Act was twice read, outside St. George's Hall and in Christian Street with up to a hundred 'rioters' being arrested. After the flight of the crowd from St. George's Plateau the disturbances centred upon Lime Street as residents behind barricades frustrated the police presence for some thirty-six hours. One city policeman eventually died from injuries received there.

In the following days more troops arrived as some 75,000 men were called out to strike when the docks were closed. Though shots were fired at night by troops near Great Homer Street, no casualties were reported.

On Thursday 15th August, two men were shot as demonstrators from a crowd of 3,000 tried to impede the passage of prison vans to Walton Gaol. In this revolutionary atmosphere a battleship and a cruiser arrived in the River Mersey and only 'suffocation by armour' seemed to prevent a serious general riot. The deep-rooted elements of class-strife were to undermine the Liverpool scene for many years to come.

To a large extent, therefore, circumstances had taken the situation beyond the control of the Chief Constable in what was an almost unparalleled episode in the history of the Town. His official connection with Liverpool, however, ceased in 1911, when he resigned and gratefully accepted a position as H.M.I. of Constabulary and he served in that position at the Home Office until 1930. Knighted in 1917, he was created a baronet in 1930.

Crowds gather to watch contingents of police and troops of the Scots Greys Regiment outside the Spekeland Road Depot, at Edge Hill Railway Station, Wavertree, during the Liverpool labour unrest, August 1911.

He returned to the Town as the necessity arose, and, in 1917, he officially came to inspect his old Force. As an advocate of the need for women police, Dunning did much to foster the Women Police Patrols in the Town. He also recognised the increased professional element amongst criminals and strongly agitated for a police college. He did much for the policemen themselves, making a distinguished contribution to the far-reaching developments which followed in the war of 1914-18, affecting the administration, conditions of service, and control of the police service in England and Wales.

Labour unrest, 1911. Thursday 15th August police and military escorts were given to food lorries and to the prison vans to Walton Gaol.

FRANCIS CALDWELL, 1912-25

A native of Liverpool's Croxteth district, Francis Caldwell was born of Scottish parents. His father was an auditor on the Staff of the Liverpool Police headquarters. His career was high-lighted by his rise from the ranks of the Force to the chief constableship.

He first entered police headquarters in 1879, as assistant clerk, working as a junior to his father. Three years later, he felt the need to familiarise himself more closely with police work and joined the Force as a constable. By 1883, he had returned to his desk as a sergeant in charge of statistics.

He rose to the rank of Inspector in 1891 and that of Superintendent in 1900. At the same time he became the confidential assistant of Chief Constable Nott Bower. When the new post of second assistant Chief Constable was created in 1896, the Watch Committee chose Caldwell as their man for the position. Following Sir Leonard Dunning's retirement from the office of Chief Constable, Caldwell succeeded him.

It was a fully justified promotion because he became a popular chief with his subordinates. He stood for efficiency and discipline, but those under his control were the first to acknowledge his fairmindedness and consideration.

Quite apart from the problems peculiar to the Great War, he had to deal with many difficult situations — the Police Strike of 1919, the Sinn Fein outrages which preceded the granting of self-government to Southern Ireland, the pre-war suffragette outrages and the post war disturbances.

The Police Strike, 1st August, 1919, however, must have caused him most personal concern. The strike resulted from longstanding grievances. As the Great War had advanced, many policemen throughout England and Wales and become embittered by the failure of their pay to rise with the cost of living. By 1918, policemen and their families had sunk so low in poverty that some were actually under-nourished, and temptations held out by bribes must at times have been irresistible. Though Whitehall made moves to alleviate the situation, it would appear that the clandestine Police Union had made up its mind that, without collective-bargaining strength, the police would not win a fair deal.

Matters came to a head in Liverpool in the Summer of 1919. Following the Strike of the London Police Force, in August 1918, the police were granted extra pay but were to be barred from striking in future. Police extremists throughout England, therefore, called for a second strike. This time they were striking for the survival of their union and not for pay. In all, some 2,364 men responded from seven forces: Metropolitan 1,056; City of London 57; Liverpool 954; Birmingham 119; Birkenhead 114; Bootle 63 and Wallasey 1. When they struck in Liverpool riots occurred, steel-helmeted troops and even tanks were sent to Merseyside, where there were bayonet charges and bloodshed. The strike collapsed after twenty-four hours, all the strikers were dismissed, and none ever reinstated. These were the agonising circumstances in which the Police Federation was born.

It was under such circumstances that the Desborough Committee had been established in March 1919. This body, fortunately, gave the decimated police forces new heart and paved the way for contentment during which the modern police service was born. So rapidly, in fact, did the Service recover that during the General Strike, in 1926, policemen throughout the country won enthusiastic praise for their bearing and impartiality. In its recommendations the Desborough Committee related the pay of the police-man — for the first time in history — to that of the semi-professional man and not that of the unskilled worker. This and other recommendations were embodied in the Police Act, 1919.

The cities and the boroughs reacted against the Desborough Committee's attempt to move towards centralization. They disliked its erosion of their right to maintain their own local police forces as they desired. It was not until 1946, however, that the smaller borough forces were abolished and the powers of the Watch Committees for appointment, promotion and discipline survived until 1964.

Caldwell remained in office, throughout a period of dramatic change in police conditions. He retired in 1925 and was presented with handsome gifts from the Force and from the Watch Committee.

As a long-standing member of the Liverpool Athenaeum, he afterwards gave much of his time to its activities.

LIONEL EVERETT, 1925-31

Born in Devon, in June 1877, Lionel Decimus Longcroft Everett joined the Wiltshire police force, at the age of eighteen. Stationed for his first eighteen months as a clerk in the office of the Chief Constable at Devizes, he also undertook daily outdoor uniformed duties in the town. Following this, he served for twelve months as a clerk in the superintendent's office at Swindon, and then did some street patrol duty. In March, 1899, he was promoted to the rank of sergeant and, in April 1902, he became an Inspector.

After eight years in Swindon, he was, in October 1905, promoted to the rank of superintendent — returning to Devizes to take charge of the Borough. This town, spreading across 86,000 acres, and housing a population of over 23,000 was divided for police purposes into three petty sessional divisions.

In May 1908, he was unanimously selected from nearly seventy applicants for the then vacant chief constableship of Preston. He settled in quickly and proved his ability to organise on a considerable scale.

When he entered the Liverpool Police Force, in 1912, as assistant chief constable, he was to begin thirteen years work in a post where his duties carried many heavy responsiblities. Throughout the Great War, he had to deal with aliens, espionage investigations, the special constabulary and the Anti-German riots. For his work in these difficult matters he was awarded an Officer-ship of the Order of the British Empire.

Together with Chief Constable, Francis Caldwell, he also participated in the anxious and exacting duties in connection with Royal visits and periods of unrest such as the race discrimination riots, the Police Strike and the Sinn Fein disturbances.

In the early part of 1930 he was awarded the King's Police Medal, and in November of the same year was invested with the insignia of the Order of St. John of Jerusalem, in recognition of the interest he had taken in first aid work and the high standards reached by Liverpool Police in this branch of their work.

ARCHIBALD WILSON, 1932-40

Archibald Wilson was born in Galston, in Ayrshire, in 1890, and was educated at Bablake, a large Midlands' public school. He passed an entrance examination to Liverpool University and intended studying veterinary science, but a family bereavement made this impossible and, in 1909, he joined the Cardiff Police Force, as a constable.

His qualities were soon appreciated and he earned rapid promotion. Whilst serving as a staff inspector at Cardiff, he was appointed, in 1928, to the chief constableship of Carlisle and the following year he was appointed to a similar position in Plymouth.

Shortly before he arrived in Liverpool, in January 1932, he bravely led a small Force of twenty policemen armed with truncheons against a mob of 200 riotous prisoners at Dartmoor and after a hand-to-hand encounter, he and his men succeeded in quelling the riot.

His eight years in Liverpool, moreover, saw him also becoming an outstanding success. Soon after his arrival, sectarian troubles came to the forefront of the Liverpool scene. Later the I.R.A. activities in the City also caused him grave concern, and it was to his credit and that of the Liverpool C.I.D. that Irish Republican activities in Liverpool were slight. In 1933 he was appointed by the Home Secretary as a member of the Departmental Committee in Detective Work and procedure.

In the same year he personally encouraged police wireless communication experiments, his men at first using Morse signals as their medium, and later direct speech. A midget receiver suitable for pedal cycles was also used and proved so successful that he eventually had it

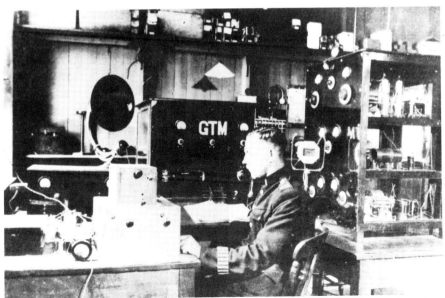

An early wireless station was completed for the city force, in 1930, at Allerton, with a range of 30 miles.

adopted for motor cycles and police cars.

When a wireless station was completed for the Force, in 1930, at Allerton, it gave the men a working radio range of thirty miles. By the outbreak of the war, in 1939, the Liverpool police had some 254 receivers at their command. Wilson also introduced a scheme whereby surrounding police forces, ranging from Warrington to Flintshire, could share in the benefit which these facilities provided.

At the request of Sir Thomas White, Wilson took control of the air raid precautions' organisation and was responsible for the creation of the Air Raid Wardens' Service, which included 12,250 members, the Auxiliary Fire Service, with an approximate strength of 5,000, and also the communications service.

A midget receiver for wireless communication proved suitable for use on police pedal cycles, c.1937.

When war first broke out he virtually lived, worked and slept for six weeks at the A.R.P. control centre in the Holt School. In March 1940, partly as a result of this unrelenting pressure of work which caused him serious eye discomfort, he was forced on medical grounds to retire from the Force.

A Commander of the Order of St. John, he held the King's Police Medal for distinguished service and in 1937, was made a Commander of the British Empire.

An official Police photograph showing one of the earliest motorcycle and sidecar combinations fitted with radio communication.

70

HERBERT WINSTANLEY, 1940-48

Herbert Winstanley, another local man to become Chief Constable of Liverpool, was born in 1885. He was educated at Liverpool Institute, won the Howard Hughes Scholarship and was awarded a school exhibition.

He embarked on a police career, in 1901, when he joined the police force as a junior clerk. Attending educational courses at University, he travelled abroad to study police methods. In so doing, he became a proficient linguist in French and Spanish.

He rose from the ranks of the Liverpool Police Force and during the Great War, 1914-18, organised aliens registration procedures for the C.I.D. — the largest of its type in the country. Many of his ideas in this field were adopted by the Home Office and were recommended to other forces. In 1920, he was awarded the M.B.E. for these services.

Chief Constable Frances Caldwell refused him leave to apply for active service because he was needed in the town. After the war he was made head of the C.I.D. and was recognised as a fingerprint expert.

Appointed Assistant Chief Constable, in 1925, he received the O.B.E. ten years later, and succeeded Archibald Wilson as Chief Constable in 1940. In this year he was awarded the King's Police Medal for "skill and conspicuous devotion to duty."

His work for Liverpool during the Second World War, 1939-45, was outstanding. In particular, he showed great ability in organising the Civil Defence. This was indeed fortunate because at the beginning of the war little detailed preparation had been accomplished in the sphere of civil defence.

For several years, prior to its commencement, the Police Force had been responsible for the special training needed for anti-gas exercises, air-raid precautions and the training of fire guards and incident officers. Fortunately for the port, the early raids on Liverpool were not severe but they did show that in many respects the City was ill-prepared and under-supplied. It was not until after the big raids, for example, that the National Fire Service was established and supplies were provided on a lavish scale. Hence, at first, many of the crews — coming to the town's assistance from beyond the Borough — were very inexperienced in dealing with serious fires.

A war-time police constable, 283A, in Duke Street, 1940. For several years prior to the commencement of World War II the police had been responsible for special training in civil defence.

The police too, had many problems to deal with as a result of the early raids. They had to take charge, whenever possible, at the scene of each serious incident, they had to extinguish fires, rescue people buried by debris, and move out those people living near unexploded bombs. Then, they had to divert traffic to avoid those roads blocked by debris. At the same time, about a million tons of goods, per month, was handled at the docks and routes had to be made free for its passage.

Some idea of the terrible problems created by the heavy bomb attacks in May 1941, is given in Winstanley's own account:

"For seven consecutive nights from 1st/2nd May to 7th/8th May, raids of varying intensity were delivered on Liverpool. Although most of the damage was to public buildings, churches and commercial and industrial premises, the extent of the raid can be judged from the total destruction of 4,400 houses, serious damage to 16,400 and slight damage to a further 45,000. Water mains were affected to such an extent that over 700 repairs were required, many involving up to 50 yards of piping. There were some 80 cases of damage to sewers.

Some 235 unexploded bombs were reported in the City and there were some 500 roads in the City closed to traffic. The worst night was that of 3rd/4th May during which there were over 600 incidents, many single incidents representing a large fire area. During the night some 400 fires were attended by the Fire Brigade.

— The effect was to close all access to the centre of the City from the South — West of Crown Street. All approaches to the Pierhead, except Dale Street, were denied to traffic for various causes. The main Dock Road was blocked in some eight places from the North to the South of the line of the Liverpool Docks and the alternative route at the north end of Liverpool Docks and the alternative route at the north end of Liverpool along Derby Road and Great Howard Street was also blocked. The Liverpool North Docks were cut off from the City by the Leeds and Liverpool Canal and several of the streets with bridges over the canal were also blocked. Access through Bootle was equally difficult."

Winstanley's men in fact, had to draw two cordons around the City, one at Queen's Drive, about three or four miles from the City centre; the second at the old City boundary, some two miles from the City centre. He felt his task and that of his constables would have been impossible without the willing assistance given by members of the Royal Navy, the Army, the Royal Air Force, the Home Guard and the Warden's Service. Especially valuable was the contribution made by neighbouring police forces in sending men each day, into the city to relieve the City constables.

After May, 1941, no raids of great consequence were made on Liverpool but the process of recovery was to take many years. During the serious raids, some 2,596 persons lost their lives, 2,548 were seriously injured and about 1,600 suffered slight injuries. Fortunately, under the Fire Brigade Regional Reinforcement Schemes, 123 brigades were sent to help the Port, but the police still found difficulties in answering the extra calls made on them by war. Thus, pensioned officers had to be appointed to the Police Reserve, a Police War reserve was established, and the Women's Auxiliary Police Corps was appointed, in August 1939.

Though Winstanley's organisational powers and personal efficiency were first-class the overall consequences of the war on the strength of the Liverpool Borough Force were tragic. The War extracted many of its finest constables for Military Service. By the beginning of 1946, therefore, the manpower situation was grave — the Force being markedly understaffed. After this time the gap was never significantly closed, so that by the end of 1966, the Liverpool Force was 525 constables below its authorised establishment. Once again, better pay and working condtions in nearby industries had much to do with the shortage.

Herbert Winstanley, therefore, in the face of some terrible conditions, had an outstanding record of achievement during his long police career. Retiring from the Liverpool Force, in April 1948, having been awarded the C.B.E. in January of the same year, he was succeeded by Charles C. Martin.

CHARLES C. MARTIN, 1948-58

Born at Gillingham, Kent, Charles Carnegie Martin was to join the Metropolitan Police in 1921. After training at their school he was posted to the Camberwell district, and in 1925 he was transferred to Whitehall Division, New Scotland Yard. In 1930, as a sergeant, he was transferred to the East End of London, Limehouse Station.

After further study at the Metropolitan Police College, Hendon, he was promoted to the rank of inspector, and from 1935 to 1937, served in the districts of Dalston and City Road. His knowledge of law later earned him the post of Senior Lecturer in Law and Duties at the Metropolitan Police Training School, Peel House, London.

Prior to the outbreak of the Second World War, he was appointed sub-divisional inspector at Westminster, in a district, which included Pimlico, Hyde Park Corner, Knightsbridge, Sloane Square and part of the Borough of Chelsea.

In the latter part of 1941, he became Chief Constable of Leamington Spa, and in November, 1942, Chief Constable of Southport. Four years later he became Senior Assistant Chief Constable of Liverpool. In 1948 he rose to the highest post in the Liverpool Force and remained there until his retirement in 1958.

During his term in Liverpool, he studied police methods in a number of Canadian and United States ports. As Chief Constable, he introduced many ideas, particularly in the field of communications which increased the efficiency of the Force. He recognised this was especially essential because of the shortage of police manpower. To help offset this burden, he established the police cadet scheme in 1948, his idea being to stimulate interest amongst boys aged 15-18.

As we have seen another of his outstanding achievements was the introduction in 1951, of his Juvenile Liaison Scheme — a venture which many city police officers believed helped prevent hundreds of youngsters from going to court. In 1955, he became one of the two representatives of the British Police Federation, who went as official delegates to the first United Nations Congress at Geneva on the prevention of crime and the treatment of offenders.

Hence, he undoubtedly enhanced the prestige and reputation of the Liverpool Force and tried to establish a happier relationship between the police and the public.

Awarded the C.B.E. in 1951, and knighted in 1957, he became the first H.M. Inspector of Constabulary for the North West to receive the Queen's Police Medal, in April 1967.

A Liverpool City Constable makes an important 'phone communication', c.1950. Such efficient methods became crucial during manpower shortages.

74

JOSEPH SMITH, 1958-64

Joseph W.T. Smith, a native of Liverpool, began his police career as a junior on the headquarters office staff when he left school in 1915. Serving with the Grenadier Guards in the First World War, he returned to the Force as a consable when he was demobilised.

Promoted to sergeant in 1923, he served in this capacity until 1935, when he rose to the rank of inspector. Three years later be became chief inspector and in 1946 he was promoted to superintendent. In 1950 he was appointed chief superintendent as head of the police administrative staffs.

In March 1958, shortly before being promoted to Chief Constable, he was awarded the Queen's Police Medal for outstanding devotion to the police service and extreme loyalty, courtesy and high integrity.

Keenly interested in boys' clubs and particularly in the Boys' Brigade, he made great efforts to maintain the high standards of the Juvenile Liaison Scheme. He retired in November 1964.

Once again, one of his most difficult problems was the great shortage of police man-power. By 1963, the Force was 130 constables below strength, and by the beginning of 1965 this had stretched to a defficiency of nearly 400.

The Force in fact faced the highest figures for crime in its history in 1963. Drastic action was called for, and soon after Chief Constable Smith retired, the Acting Chief Constable, Herbert Balmer —or Bert Balmer as he was popularly known — decided to implement bold new police policies.

"This is war", he declared, in November 1964, and almost immediately began to attack Liverpool's crime as a major operation, supported by the latest scientific measures. In less than two months, his Force of 2,172 police constables, mounted a four-pronged attack. In the forefront they used the most modern television and radio techniques, backing them by the formation of a plain clothes "commando squad". This consisted of 100 younger men and women handpicked from all City police divisions. Dressed as businessmen, 'layabouts', courting couples, husbands and wives, they had excellent results, especially when assisted by television and radio aids. Special meetings and briefings were then undertaken to keep all the members of the Force informed of Herbert Balmer's plans and results, and to invoke general streamlining and economising of manpower.

The immediate result of the campaign, was a 25 per cent reduction of crime in the City and a vast increase in the rate of detections. The week beginning 28th December, 1964, had the lowest crime figures for the previous eighteen months. In 'A' Division, an area of the town where the "commando squad" operated and where shop-breakings and thefts from cars had always been rife, detections were credited against 57.3 per cent of the crimes committed in one week.

Appointed as Acting Chief Constable in November 1964, Balmer did not qualify under Home Office regulations to be permanently awarded the chief constableship. The Home Office insisted that all chief constables must have served at least two years at a rank above inspector in another Force. Herbert Balmer had spent all his thirty-eight police years in the Liverpool Force.

His achievements after such a short period of command in the Borough were soon recognised by many members of the public and they called for his retention. This, however, was not to be.

JAMES HAUGHTON, 1965-67

Lancashire-born James Haughton, an experienced police officer, was appointed to succeed Joseph Smith as head constable of Liverpool in June 1965. He was promoted to the position whilst serving as assistant Chief Constable of Staffordshire, and was on secondment to the Home Office Police Research and Planning Branch at that time. His period of office as head of the Liverpool City Force was to be short, for in April 1967, the Constabulary amalgamated with that of nearby Bootle. In turn, however, he became the first chief of the enlarged Force.

A native of Oldham, James Haughton had been a policeman for thirty years before he took his first Liverpool post. He began his career as a constable in the Birmingham Police Force and had risen to Detective Chief Superintendent and head of the C.I.D. by the time he left for Staffordshire in 1961. Whilst head of the Birmingham C.I.D. he held the distinguished record of not having a single unsolved murder case during his period as chief.

His most famous Midlands' case involved a seven week investigation into the death of a young woman who was decapitated and mutilated at a Birmingham Y.W.C.A. hostel, two days before Christmas 1959. The accused, a Warrington man who had been working in Birmingham, was eventually convicted of manslaughter and sentenced to life imprisonment.

James Haughton left Birmingham to become Assistant Chief Constable of Staffordshire, in 1961, and was seconded to the Home Office Police Research and Planning Branch two years later.

During this term at the Home Office he travelled extensively studying police methods on the Continent and in the United States and Canada.

Using his experience with the Midland Regional Crime Squad, he played a major part in organising similar squads throughout the country, and he also encouraged adjacent police authorities to co-operate in patrolling Motorway roads.

He studied the use of computers for police records and fingerprints and the use of machines for teaching policemen new scientific techniques. Much of the work in organising the new Liverpool and Bootle Police Force, fell to him. He was appointed H.M. Chief Inspector of Constabulary in January 1976; knighted in The New Year's Honours List, he retired in December 1977.

Part Five

AMALGAMATION
AND
THE MERSEYSIDE POLICE FORMATION

AMALGAMATION AND
THE MERSEYSIDE POLICE FORMATION

When Liverpool's citizens witnessed the last patrols of their city constables, in 1967, another era in provincial police history had come to a close. The Liverpool borough policemen and policewomen joined with those of nearby Bootle to form an amalgamated force. In 1974, these constables became part of an even larger police administrative unit, the Merseyside Police Force. James Haughton, who so ably led both the Liverpool city and the amalgamated force, of 1967, maintained his position as chief constable throughout these changes until 1975. He was succeeded by Kenneth Oxford who remained as Chief Constable until his retirement in 1989.

Those citizens who did object to having their own local police force absorbed into a larger, regional police unit, took their stand against a complex, long-term process. This fundamental trend in police administration had been evolving since 1854 in keeping with those ideas suggested by the then Home Secretary, Lord Palmerston.

Much of the ground work for 'model policing' in the provinces had been established before the eighteen fifties by the better organised police forces, such as that in Liverpool. When the Liverpool Watch Committee established a borough force, in 1836, its members took a decisive step against crime in the North West of England. Several other nearby police forces, which had been formed much later, came to look on the Liverpool police

The ultra-modern Merseyside Police Headquarters, Canning Place, Liverpool, opened by H.M. The Queen 4 May 1982. The H.Q. overlooks the prestigious Albert Dock complex and is situated in the district where Victorian policemen, armed with cutlasses, faced mobs of rioters in the 1840's.

force as an 'ideal model' and, in times of emergency, one to seek help from. Liverpool policemen had in fact, in the Victorian age, assisted in the nearby townships of Crosby, Southport, St Helens and Birkenhead.

Until the Liverpool constables established themselves as respected law-enforcers in the locality an outstanding number of criminals had virtually had a 'free hand'. Law-breaking in the port itself was accepted by many as a right and thousands flagrantly flouted the law. Traditions of public violence, mob-rule, gross intemperance, foul language and open sexual immorality became regarded as acceptable behaviour, by some.

The new Liverpool constabulary, following the lead of Sir Robert Peel's metropolitan police force, employed several former London police officers, but still had serious weaknesses. Liverpool's head constables were often restricted by the rulings of the watch committee, by the local magistrates, by the pressure from political parties and by the continual shortage of qualified manpower.

The failure of the head constables to overcome the latter problem, throughout almost the entire history of the Liverpool force, meant that the men from the lower ranks, in particular, had to undertake excessive periods of duty and they also received very poor pay. Though their wages notably improved after the recommendations of the Desborough Committee, 1919, the men again faced serious shortages of personnel after the Second World War. At the termination of the Liverpool City Force their shortages had stretched to a total of more than 20 per cent of their establishment. James Haughton thereby found it impossible, in 1965, to implement regulation 23 (2) of the police regulations of that year granting seven days rest in each four weekly period of duty undertaken by the lower ranked constables. Liverpool's 'bobbies' had to be content, at best, with six days of leave.

Their excessive hours, in part, stemmed from the new duties continually being forced upon them. As local urban expansion accelerated, the Liverpool men were forced to move further and further beyond their original parish boundaries. In their earliest years they witnessed large adjacent districts in Everton and West Derby, for example, being added to their territory. In 1895 they had Walton, Wavertree and the larger part of Old Swan added. Early in the twentieth century, they took over responsibility for Garston, for Fazackerley, for Childwall and for Woolton and Much Woolton.

This type of expansion had been encouraged in the provinces by a succession of Home Secretaries supporting the Palmerston ideal. Some of their cumulative efforts had, for example, helped to win a majority of members of parliament to support the Local Government Bill of 1888. After this legislation became law, those police forces which operated within a township with a population of less than 10,000 citizens had to face amalgamation with other local police forces.

Additional factors, too, such as the exigencies of the twentieth century's Great Wars, served only to accentuate this trend. Reformers, quite justifiably it would seem, called for greater emphasis on the national need to deploy constables efficiently in wartime. A further major consequence was the introduction of the Police Bill, in 1946, which eventually led to the disappearance of more splendid police forces.

By the early sixties other respected local police forces, including those of Bootle, Southport, Birkenhead and St. Helens — which eventually came to form part of the

Merseyside Police Force — increasingly came under threat. Those persons supporting the retention of these hitherto independent forces argued that they had distinguished histories worthy of comparison with the largest police forces in the North West.

Those men and women who composed such local forces faced an alarming rise in the seriousness of the threats to their health and safety. At this time, too, our local constables began to receive mounting publicity for their plight from several sources. Their relationship with the public, in common with those of other forces throughout the United Kingdom, also began to attract growing concern. Both national and local newspaper reporters increasingly seized upon any isolated incident that seemed to impugn the good name of the police service.

Meanwhile, not only the Liverpool and Bootle constables, but a vast number of other policemen and women throughout England and Wales, reached a major turning point after years of uncertainty about their future. When a royal commission eventually took up its appointment, in 1960, it was pressed to seek answers not only to manpower weaknesses but also to the widespread rise in reported crimes and to the ever-increasing dangers arising from the unprecedented growth in the volume of road traffic and the problems that accompanied this.

Overworked police constables, particularly those in Liverpool and Bootle, needed immediate help. In plain terms, their conditions of service — especially their pay — had to be made immediately more attractive. The commissioners vehemently argued their case for a suitable pay formula that would take into account the social and industrial changes that had occurred since the end of the Second World War in 1945.

In his excellent analysis, T.A. Critchley has summarised how the commissioners, in their interim report, met the police officers' claim almost in full. In their final report, in May 1962, the commissioners also went on to take up the case again for greater national unity within the police service. They also dismissed, though not with unanimity, the claim that a more national style of police force might lead to a 'police state'.

In turn the Police Act of June 1964 comprehensively revised the whole general body of law regarding the administration of our provincial police forces. It made an emphatic attempt, too, to define the role of the Home Secretary, that of the local police authorities and that of their chief constables. Each of the latter was thereafter given more explicit control over his own policemen. Significantly, too, a police officer no longer faced being confined solely to the jurisdiction of the district under the charge of his local chief constable. Chief police officers, too, could enter into greater collaboration with the heads of other police forces. As T.A. Critchley accurately recorded, by the time this Police Act came into force in its entirety, in June 1965, a 'national police service', consisting of loosely federated units, had taken shape.

Quite naturally, many citizens of both Liverpool and Bootle attempted to forcibly air their views regarding the proposed amalgamation of 1967. At a national level, however, parliamentarians appeared to become increasingly frustrated when attempting to have their questions answered regarding provincial policing matters.

Local politicians had never before been confronted by the prospect of the Home Office exercising the type of control over their police forces that it had hitherto exerted over the

Metropolitan Police Force. Local reaction to proposed police mergers and the increasing power sought over police forces by the Home Secretary, Roy Jenkins, was often blunt. In nearby Southport, for example, his proposal, in 1967, that the Southport Borough force should be joined to the Lancashire County Constabulary was dismissed in a meeting of the members of the Southport Watch Committee that lasted only ten minutes. Liverpool city councillors for their part, in January 1967 had decided, in a marathon meeting to protest to the Home Secretary regarding the administrative proposals for the joint Liverpool-with-Bootle Police Force. The movement towards national police unity, however, was not to be halted.

National and local newspaper reporters at the same time did not defuse, and probably inflamed, the situation with a demand for a 'War on Crime'. In Liverpool in 1966, thieves stole property the reported total value of which exceeded £1,000,000 for the first time in the seaport's history. By December 1969 some local city reporters declared Liverpool to be facing a 'wave of terror' from the users of drink, drugs, knives, razors and fire-arms. All such headlines served to polarise the attention of newspaper readers throughout the Merseyside region and pressed them into supporting new initiatives for overcoming the excesses of those persons engaged in 'open' criminal activity.

They, like other British citizens, were encouraged to express their worries and doubt concerning the mechanism for bringing police officers to account for any questionable behaviour. It was against this background that the larger, regional Merseyside Police Force was formed.

The new Merseyside Police Force, in the long term, resulted from the fundamental evolutionary process of the police service outlined above. The new Metropolitan local government districts, in the short term, prepared the ground for the introduction of such forces in 1974.

Though a full, in-depth analysis of the Force's formation and the contribution of the Force and its officers to the police service is not possible within the scope of this book, hopefully it will be undertaken in the future. The Force is still very much in its infancy when compared to the one hundred and thirty year history of the Liverpool Police Force and painstaking research into the contribution of the other original, component forces will necessarily have to be made. However, a brief survey of the development of the Merseyside Police Force would indicate that it has continued to build upon the finest elements of the established provincial police service. Two outstanding chief constables to date, Sir James Haughton and Sir Kenneth Oxford, appear to have surmounted considerable obstacles to rapidly give the Force a distinctive, modern identity. Newly appointed Chief Constable James Sharples, too, would appear — in view of his appointment to lead the police 'Guildford Four' inquiry — to possess that high degree of personal integrity, professional resourcefulness and unswerving sense of resolution so necessary to lead a modern metropolitan police command.

Chief Constable James Haughton must be accredited with achieving the 1974 'changeover' with the minimum of disturbance, particularly to the public and all those local officers and their families who were involved. He began the process of assimilating any differences in the methods of policing used by the component forces which formed the new force. This he did still facing the financial restrictions and the manpower shortages inherited from the three amalgamated districts of Cheshire, Lancashire (Sefton, Knowsley and St. Helens) and Liverpool — with Bootle which came to compose the Merseyside Force. As he so aptly observed, in 1974, for many constables and their families this was the second major upheaval since 1967 and many must have viewed it with apprehension; "the only constant element in the police service has been 'change' and even this seems to have gone into overdrive in recent months".

He and his constables had to face such up-heavals at a period when they also had to confront the criminal activities of vandals, those causing disorder in public places, absconding juvenile delinquents, illegal drugs-users and those using fire-arms and shot-guns. Merseyside was especially plagued by the high incidence of criminals engaged in robberies, noteably where fire-arms had been used, and where crimes against the person — particularly those carrying cash whilst on business — were widespread.

In addition, James Haughton showed concern over those criminals carrying out a high number of burglaries and attacks on safes, or valuable cargoes in lorries or trailers. He and his senior officers also expressed their anxiety regarding the growth of 'typical offences' of violence on lonely persons — many elderly. Those vicious and cowardly persons carrying out such robberies joined the bands of masked and armed thugs increasingly attacking the staff of public houses, post offices and licensed betting offices. He also noted the growing number of persons resorting to fraud.

At the same time he and his officers became appalled by the growth in numbers of those children apparently destined for a life of crime. Several engaged firstly, in 'fringe activities' such as the organising of gangs to meet, after school hours, in 'warfare.' Particularly lamentable was the need to arrest and re-arrest some juveniles resorting to theft or robbery. This situation he attributed to the delays caused in bringing the accused to trial. At this period, too, Merseyside traffic officers had to confront the growth in 'hit and run' motor vehicle incidents and the growing numbers of law-breakers engaged in 'auto crimes', or car thefts. Those resorting to such deplorable activities, often children in fact, accounted in total for some 30.7 per cent of the Force's 'crime load' when they effectively took charge of these lethal motorised weapons often caused the maimings and even the deaths of innocent Merseysiders.

Not surprisingly, local police officers welcomed the opportunity to use the newly-introduced stolen-vehicle index of the Police National Computer. Further concern about national criminal trends, also began to be voiced by local policemen concerned with the spread of terrorist activity and the growing illegal use of 'controlled drugs'.

When James Haughton resigned in 1975, having been appointed H.M. Chief Inspector of Constabulary, he expressed his high regard for those law-abiding citizens of Merseyside who had so willingly assisted him and his Force. He was able to record his thanks for the opportunity given to his men to be actively involved with the Merseyside Structure Plan and the key issues of homes, jobs, transport facilities and leisure amenities it incorporated. Looking to the future of the Force he was pleased to express the importance in the marked growth, at last, of those applying for employment in the local police service. With foresight, too, he noted the growing emergence of 'some irresponsible, mischievous, malicious or indeed subversive groups of people who make unwarranted and unsubstantiated criticisms or accusations against members of the police service.' His conclusion that 'this is dangerous for society' was to be even more widely supported by his successor, Kenneth Oxford.

Following a year as deputy chief constable for Merseyside, the man who was eventually to be knighted for his sterling police service Kenneth Oxford, began his term as Chief Constable in 1975. A strong-willed, firm-handed police officer, he sought from the beginning of his term in office to establish the Merseyside Police Force as one 'for the wrongdoer to respect and reckon with and for the people of Merseyside to be proud of'. Forever forward-looking in his approaches to policing he, too, as other Liverpool-based police officers in the past, had to remain intrepid and unnerved in the face of a series of crises that questioned the fundamental integrity and honesty of purpose of his force.

From the start he sought to bring the strength of the force up to the 5,600 constables which had been recommended as an ideal establishment figure. He felt that the 4,317 constables available left him with a somewhat 'threadbare situation'. This, in turn, led to many shortcomings in the effective policing of Merseyside. He vigorously continued to press for a redress by a series of meaningful discussions with the local County Executive, the Home Office and the H.M. Inspectorate representatives.

Local public disquiet at the rise in criminal statistics, meanwhile, appeared to be centred upon those for the crimes of violence. Crimes of vandalism, ie. violent attacks on property, seemed to most influence public opinion. He reported these to have risen, in 1977, by 59.5 per cent and felt they did most to intrude upon the everyday life of local people. Serious upset, again, was being voiced by those members of the public worried about the increasing number of reported vicious attacks. Local attacks by females, for example, also seemed to be following the national trend of 'being on the increase'. 'Muggers', especially, attracted media coverage although their actual proportionate number of violent offences was low.

By comparison, those engaged in robbery on Merseyside appeared to be almost two and one half times greater in number that the national average for 1977. Other features of local crime that continued to cause concern included those persons involved with shop lifting, joy-riding in stolen vehicles, drunken-driving and 'battered wives' and 'battered children'. Violent crime for Kenneth Oxford was especially disturbing in relation to licensed premises. More young people, he believed, appeared to be encouraged to drink heavily in some of the Liverpool city centre night clubs.

Local police activities to curtail such abuses of the licensing laws were liable to attract the anxious attention of the public when seized upon by those described as 'investigative journalists'. In the face of a series of incidents, at a national level, which questioned the accountability of chief police officers at this time, Kenneth Oxford was pleased to announce that he felt for his part he enjoyed 'a healthy, realistic and professional relationship' with his police authority. To his credit, whenever necessary, he was able to maintain the enthusiasm, morale and professional dedication of his constables in the face of several prolonged bouts of hostile criticism. This stand he regarded as absolutely vital, for example, following the death of James Kelly, in 1979, in custody in Huyton Police Station and the ensuing media 'sensationalism'.

In July and August, in the following year, the officers of the Merseyside Force had to experience a series of riots in the Toxteth district of Liverpool. These came in the wake of serious outbreaks of public disorder in London and other major cities. The Toxteth Riots perhaps compared in intensity of mob violence, to that experienced by Liverpool constables under the leadership of Michael Whitty, Matthew Dowling, John Greig, Leonard Dunning and Francis Caldwell. With violence against property and against the police themselves reaching an intolerable pitch, in the early morning hours of 6th July 1980, the Chief Constable reluctantly directed C.S. Gas to be used for the first time on the streets of England. By this time, with 282 police officers already injured and others being subjected to an intense barrage of petrol bombs, metal stakes and missiles of every nature, he, like other chief constables in similar circumstances, had no alternative but to prevent a further series of injuries to his officers and widespread destruction of the city of Liverpool.

The dramatic events occurred as concern was also being voiced in public regarding the work of the Special Branch in the Liverpool district. He attempted to allay any fears by a brief description of the formation of a Liverpool Port Unit of the Special Branch, in answer to the escalation of Irish terrorist activity both in Ireland and the British mainland. Essentially he described how the officers engaged were to screen the heavy number of passengers that travelled, via the airport or ferry terminals, between these countries. All such officers he re-affirmed were liable to follow the Police Discipline Code and were accountable to him and his senior officers.

Despite the excessive pressure from such burdens, he continued with his aim of stream-lining the Merseyside Police Force. He initiated, for example, the development of the new post of Chief Superintendent of Operations within the Force. His Mangagement and Computer Project Team, formed in the mid seventies furthermore, carried out a comprehensive survey of the Force. This team of officers received training to familiarise themselves with the principal police computer systems involving documentation procedure and the collation, selection, recording, presentation and analysis of vital data. As a direct result of this review, the Chief Constable was able to introduce a new system of Merseyside Police Orders for commencement on 1st January 1978.

At the same time he encouraged his officers to take a leading role in local community life and he insisted that they play their full part in the 'Merseyside . . . Into the Eighties with Pride', initiative. In this he planned that he and his men should make their contribution to help solve as many problems confronting the local community as possible. He was especially concerned to help the youth of the area.

His concern for the community and his police officers' role within it remained a feature of his ideals until his retirement — after thirteen years' service — from the post of Chief Constable. His achievements and that of his fellow officers cannot be fully and adequately described within the scope of this chapter. Hopefully, at some later date, a full account of the merits of the Merseyside Police Force will be undertaken.

Thanks in part to his efforts and those of his senior officers, however, Merseysiders were able to face the 'Eighties with pride and, towards the end of the decade, with a new found sense of confidence. With more police officers being made available, whenever possible, for foot or cycle patrols — linked to a vehicle support system — a traditional approach to the management of the Force began to re-emerge in the mid Eighties. This essentially stemmed from the 1983 publication of the statement of 'The Aims of the Merseyside Police Force', after discussions with the Police Committee, the H.M. Chief Inspectorate of Constabulary, the senior Mersey police officers, the police staff associations and, importantly, the general public.

From this point all the constables of the Force were directed to channel their policing energies into, firstly, the traditional aims of the police service and, secondly, those goals regarded by their sub-division commanders as most vital to their own local community. Each sub-division officer generally proceeded with six broad aims, namely to encourage closer relationships between the local communities and the police; to involve the community in crime-prevention and self-help programmes; to control the trafficking of hard drugs with an emphasis on education, treatment and rehabilitation; to secure better standards of driver behaviour and improve the road worthiness of vehicles through a vehicle rectification scheme; to develop the professionalism of the police so that every citizen be treated in a civil and sensitive manner; to ensure the operational efficiency of each police department. These, briefly, were those goals of 1988. Kenneth Oxford had amended them in light of police experience in the earlier eighties.

Merseyside's police officers managed to achieve a marked growth of co-operation in many local communities after they introduced the Home Watch Scheme of 1983. By 1986 a total of 2,500 local schemes had been formed. Community forums, introduced by the chief constable in response to the Scarman Report, were to be seen to work alongside meetings with parish councils and other liaisons as essential ingredients to remove the fear of crime in the locality. In some districts, the police themselves contributed, where possible, with their own local, organised responses to special pleas for help. The Neighbourhood Constable Scheme of Speke, the Wavertree Road Home Beat Officer, the Neighbourhood Beat Officers at Huyton and the Area Community Officers at Copy Lane were typical of such responses. Increasing liaison with school children in the form of the Schools' Contact Programmes were also organised.

Throughout the Eighties growing police concern for drug trafficking, as a serious social problem, usually met with well-supported public responses. Drug Squad officers noted that heroin became more readily available yet believed cannabis and cannabis resin became the drugs most easily obtained in the County. As a part-reply to the growing problem the Regional Crime Squad officers established a Dedicated Drugs Unit and Merseyside police assisted it by sending experienced officers — from their Central Drug Squad — as their own squad numbers increased in 1985 and 1986. Though the Merseyside drugs' squad officers believed it was always difficult to accurately quantify the drugs problem they believed a 'levelling off' in growth began to occur about this time. Users and traffickers, nevertheless, they discovered, became much more subtle in their means of distribution. Some for example resorted to the 'dial-a-smack' ring of Wirral. In this the users, when calling a given phone number would be told of a location, to buy their drugs.

Other users increasingly concealed their drugs, by swallowing them pre-wrapped in 'cling film' if challenged. Despite such desperate behaviour, police officers and H.M. officers of Customs and Excise achieved some noteworthy seizures of concealed drugs in transit at local docks. By 1988 a 30.6 per cent increase in seizures had been achieved, over the previous year. Major initiatives to combat the newly discovered scourge of A.I.D.S. were also introduced.

As indicated earlier, the crime-load of those police officers engaged with standards of road-drivers' behaviour was immense. These officers in effect found that crimes involving vehicles still represented about 30 per cent of all recorded crime in 1987. However, the incidence of theft and reckless driving of high powered motor-vehicles appeared to come more and more to the fore. This development eventually initiated the introduction of a helicopter on a trial basis and showed great promise in reducing the often tragic consequences of this form of theft. Some 20 children, for example, met with death in road accidents in 1983. Throughout the Eighties the severest forms of 'the bull in the china shop' approach to driving offences continued to enrage many Merseysiders. Police attention was persistently directed to parking on pavements, or in awkward places, to traffic light 'jumping', the careless abandoning of vehicles and the excessive speed of drivers in narrow, congested streets.

Kenneth Oxford and his senior officers, nevertheless, continued unwaveringly to emphasize the need to maintain a high level of professionalism in their constables. As seen above, he was always keen to involve as many non-police agencies as possible to help with this policy. This was achieved in the face of even the most trying of social upheaval. Both nationally and on Merseyside, a growing number of persons still appeared to be prepared to use violence gratuitously, often against the weak and the elderly, for paltry gains. In some Merseyside districts not only police officers but shop-keepers, insurance collectors, priests, doctors and nurses became regularly subjected to violent attacks.

Members of the Force meanwhile, continued to confront additional demands on their resources. In the mid Eighties the introduction of the Police and Criminal Evidence Act necessitated re-training that led to the loss of some 15,000 man/days equivalent to the withdrawal of sixty-six constables for a full year. In response to such burdens the Chief Constable continuously sought to remove the apparently ever-growing bureaucratic demands on his constables that might prevent their greater contact with the communities.

At senior officer level he continued to encourage his staff to take full advantage of sophisticated computer systems to improve efficiency, whenever possible, at the expense of the old manual procedures. His ideas attracted the attention of other United Kingdom policemen and that of the chiefs of overseas police forces, from as far afield as Queensland and South Australia. His planning extended, in time, to the 'back-recording' of criminal records on a computerised system. In turn, he was able to claim that Merseyside Police Force was the first in the United Kingdom with an integrated Command-and-Control and criminal record system. The Force had in effect completed the long journey from cutlasses to computers.

When he retired from his command in 1989 the Merseyside police force, with 4,685 constables and some 2000 civilian personnel had a distinctively modern identity. This was a remarkable achievement for such a relatively young police unit. Comparisons with the earlier, local forces such as the Liverpool-with-Bootle Force are difficult, if not impossible, fairly to undertake. However, some of the high standards of the members of the new force are perhaps reflected in the fact that only two of its members faced dismissal in 1988. In some of the Victorian years, as many as 20 per cent of the Liverpool Force were reported for serious offences, mainly drunkenness, as constables fell to the numerous temptations of that era.

By the end of the nineteen eighties a high per centage of constables had received commendations or awards — far too numerous to be detailed here. They were worthy of recording and were presented in the chief constables' annual reports from 1974 to 1988. The men and women of the force — and their families — consistently helped to raise funds for noteworthy charities. Outstanding achievements by the constables ranged from remarkable bravery in rescuing endangered persons in burning homes to representing the British Police Service in the European Cross Country Championships in Switzerland.

Perhaps the most symbolic form of help from Merseyside Police Force officers came in the meticulous arrangements they made for the nineteen Royal visits to the area in 1988. Having, in 1984, safeguarded the visit of Her Majesty, The Queen, and H.R.H. the Duke of Edinburgh, to Merseyside — for the opening of the International Garden Festival and the Queen Elizabeth II Law Courts and for the review of the tall Ships Parade in the River Mersey — the local police officers prepared to safeguard H.R.H. the Prince of Wales on 24th May 1988.

On this occasion Prince Charles visited the Albert Dock complex and re-opened the refurbished warehouses which included the Tate Gallery. Merseyside police officers were able to co-ordinate their security arrangements from their ultra-modern, central headquarters in Canning Place, which faced the Albert Dock complex. By comparison, when Prince Albert had originally opened the Dock, in July 1846, the head constable of Liverpool, Maurice Dowling, had been able to prepare his excellent arrangements from the then dock police headquarters in nearby James Street. Unlike the modern environment of the Albert Dock, however this district of Canning Place in Liverpool, in the eighteen forties was a hot-bed of crime. Hordes of wrongdoers sought out the penny-ale cellars, the bawdy singing saloons, the gambling dens and the sleazy 'theatres' and the like that infested the waterfront.

As we have seen above, in the face of violent mobs, our Victorian policemen — particularly in the 1830's and 1840's — had sometimes to protect themselves and local property with cutlasses. To these early policemen, and to their Merseyside successors, those who cherish basic civilized standards of behaviour are today indebted. If members of the contemporary public can help today's police officers then life for all sections of the community will not become 'fearful and miserable'. Life for those in the police service, at the same time, will no longer be the 'dangerous, difficult and thankless task', that James Haughton felt it sometimes could become.

In spite of the decline in the volume of trade and in the number of ships passing through the seaport of Liverpool in recent years, the distinctive problems of local crime are immense. One can be sure that the members of our Merseyside Police Force will continue to cope with the increasing demands that are made upon them. Like their predecessors they are ever-willing to employ new technology and to continue the long and honourable police service traditions handed down to them. They police the localities of Merseyside, efficiently, compassionately and with insight and intelligence. Liverpudlians and indeed Merseysiders in general can be justly proud of their local guardians of law and order past and present.

SELECT BIBLIOGRAPHY OF PRINTED SOURCES

I Manuscript Sources

Much of this type of material was obtained from the Liverpool Record Office — the records of the Commissioners of Watch, Scavengers and Lamps, and those of the Watch Committee (1836-1902) being the most important. These records have been summarily listed in the Classified List of Corporation Records in the Liverpool Record Office, to which reference should be made.

II Parliamentary and Departmental Papers

1. Select Committee on Drunkenness, p.p. 1834 viii.

2. Royal Commission on Municipal Corporations in England and Wales, First Report, p.p. 1835 xxiii.

3. Royal Commission on the establishment of a Constabulary Force in England and Wales, First Report p.p. 1839 xvii.

4. Royal Commission on the Health of Towns; First Report p.p. 1844 xvii.

5. Select Committee on the Expediency of adopting a more uniform system of police in England and Wales and Scotland. First Report, p.p. 1852-53.

6. Select Committee on Public Houses, p.p. 1854 xiv.

7. Select Committee on the Contagious Diseases Bill, p.p. 1866 xi.

8. Select Committee on police superannuation funds, p.p. 1875 xiii.

9. Select Committee on Metropolitan Fire Brigade, p.p. 1876 xi.

10. Royal Commission on the Penal Servitude Acts, p.p. 1878-79 Vol. I & II xxxvii; Vol. III xxxviii.

11. Select Committee on the Contagious Diseases Acts, 1866-69 p.p. 1880 viii: 1881 viii: 1882 ix.

12. Prevention of Crimes Act, 1871. Amendment p.p. 1884-85 iv.

The Annual reports of Her Majesty's Inspectors of Constabulary, 1857-1897.
The Annual reports of the Government Inspectors of Prisons, 1836-1878.
The Annual reports of the chief constables of Liverpool, 1836-1967.
The Annual reports of the Chief Constable of Merseyside, 1975-1989.

BOOKS AND ARTICLES

J. H. Bagot, *Juvenile Delinquency* (1941)

T. Baines, *History of the Commerce of Liverpool* (1952)

T. C. Barker & J. R. Harris, *St. Helens 1750-1900* (1959)

G. V. Blackstone, *A History of the British Fire Service* (1957)

A. Briggs, *Victorian Cities* (1964)

T. A. Critchley, *A History of Police in England and Wales, 1900-1966* (1967)

C. Dickens, *The Uncommercial Traveller* (1860)

F. Engels, *The Condition of the Working Class in England in 1844* (1892)

S. E. Finer, *The Life and Times of Sir Edwin Chadwick* (1952)

W. M. Frazer, *Duncan of Liverpool* (1947)

J. L. and B. Hammond, *James Stansfield* (1932 ed.)

J. Hart (i) *Reform of the Borough Police 1835-56 English Historical Review*, Vol. LXX July, 1955.
(ii) The County and Borough Police Act, 1856. *Journal of Public Administration,* Vol. XXXIV, Winter 1956, p.405.

J. M. Hart, *The British Police* (1951)

F. Henriques, *Prostitution and Society*, Vol. III (1968)

E. W. Hope (i) *Health at the Gateway* (1931), (ii) Police and Fire Brigade *Public Health Congress Handbook* (1903)

Q. Hughes, *Seaport: Architecture and townscape in Liverpool* (1964)

S. Hugill, *Sailortown* (1967)

H. Jones, *Crime in a Changing Society* (1965)

J. O. Jones, *The History of the Caernarvonshire Constabulary, 1856-1950* (1963)

M. Lee, *A History of Police in England* (1901)

P. Magnus, *Gladstone* (1954)

S. E. Matlby, *Manchester and the Movement for National Elementary Education* (1918)

C. L. Mowat, *Britain between the Wars, 1918-40* (1964 Ed.)

J. W. Nott Bower, *Fifty-two years a policeman* (1926)

J. Ord, *Origins and History of the Glasgow Police Force* (1906)

T. Kelly, *Adult Education in Liverpool* (1960)

H. Parris, The Home Office and the Provincial Police in England and Wales, 1856-70 *Public Law* (Spring 1961)

H. Pelling, *A History of British Trade Unionism* (1963)

J. A. Picton, *Memorials of Liverpool Vol. II* (1903 Ed.)

G. H. Pumphrey, *Liverpool Public Services* (1940)

L. Radzinowicz, *A History of English Criminal Law*, Vol. III (1956) and Vol. IV (1968)

E. F. Rathbone, *The Rise and Progress of Liverpool 1551-1831* (1910)

C. Reith, *A short History of the British Police* (1948)

R. B. Rose, "John Finch, 1784-1857: A Liverpool Discipline of Robert Owen". Reprinted from the *Transactions of the Historic Society of Lancashire and Cheshire*, Vol. 107 (1967)

A. G. L. Shaw, *Convicts and Colonies (1966)*

H. Shimmin, *Liverpool Life*. Its pleasures, practices and pastimes (1856 and 1857)

M. Simey, *Charitable Effort in Nineteenth Century Liverpool* (1951)

J. J. Tobias, *Crime and Industrial Society in the Nineteenth Century* (1967)

A. Solmes, *The English Policeman* (1935)

J. Tonjeau, *The Rise and Progress of Liverpool, 1551-1835* (1910)

P. J. Waller, *Democracy and Sectarianism: A political and social history of Liverpool 1868-1939* (1981)

H. W. Walmsley, *The Life of Sir Joshua Walmsley* (1879)

S. and B. Webb (i) *English Local Government. Manor and the Borough* (1908 Ed.) (ii) *Industrial Democracy*, Vol. I (1897) (iii) *The History of Liquor Licensing in England* (1903 Ed.) (iv) *English Prisons under Local Government*

B. D. White, *History of the Corporation of Liverpool, 1835-1914* (1951)

P. T. Winskill and J. Thomas, *Temperance Movement in Liverpool and District, 1829-87* (1887)

A. F. Young and E. T. Ashton, *British Social Work in the Nineteenth Century* (1956)

Dictionary of National Biography Vol. LII (1897) and Vol. LXI (1900)

The following are some of the most important newspapers and articles consulted:
A. Nineteenth Century.
i. Liverpool Citizen, 5th December, 1888.
ii. Liberal Review, 25th May, 1878.
iii. Liverpool Review, 19th January 1884, 2nd February 1884, 16th March 1889

B. Twentieth Century.
i. Catholic Pictorial, 11th December 1966.
ii. London Illustrated News, 16th January, 1965.
iii. Police and Crime, Bound volumes of newspaper cuttings in the Liverpool Record Office, 1931-1965.

APPENDIX 1. Some Significant Dates and Developments.

1835   The Municipal Corporations Act enables the Liverpool Councillors to elect a Watch Committee.

1836   The town watchmen and corporation constables are united — the dock constabulary remains independent — with Michael Whitty as the first Head Constable. He also takes charge of the borough, part-time fire constables.

1841   The dock and town constabulary are united. The central dock police station is in James Street.

1843   A warehouse constables' unit is formed.

1846   Liverpool's first chief of detectives is appointed.

1856   Liverpool Police Force is declared 'in admirable order' by H.M.I. of Constabulary.

ʼc.1859 Charles Dickens enlists as a Liverpool 'special' constable.

1865   The River Police Department is established.

1868   The Police Band is formed.

1872   A telegraph system for the fire-stations is introduced.

1879   Infantry and dragoons assist the police during the dock labourers' strike.

1881   Liverpool policemen frustrate Fenian attempts to dynamite the town hall and the police section-house.

1881   The police fire-brigade make use of the telephone.

1884   The first horse-drawn ambulance is introduced by the Watch Committee.

1886   The Mounted Police Department is formed.

1890   25,000 march to support the dockers' strike. Infantry are stationed inside the docks to assist the police.

1890   All the bridewells are linked by telephone to the main bridewell.

1891   Police horse-drawn patrol wagons are introduced.

1895   The Liverpool and Bootle Police Orphanage is opened.

1901   Petroleum-powered fire-engines are introduced.

1911   Liverpool police receive military assistance during the transport workers' strike which includes 'Bloody Sunday'.

1917   The Chief Constable sanctions voluntary women's patrols.

1919   The Police Strike.

1920   Traffic policemen patrol on motor-cycle 'combinations'.

1921   The Explosives and Fire Prevention Department is established.

1933   Police vehicles use experimental wirelesses.

1939   The Women's Auxiliary Police Corps is appointed.

1939-1945 Liverpool becomes a 'number one' port. Police control civil defence and air-raid precautions.

1941	Liverpool police fire-brigade duties are adopted by the National Fire Service.
1947	The Liverpool City Police-Women's Corps is established.
1948	The Police Cadet Corps is established.
1951	The Liverpool Juvenile Liaison Scheme is introduced.
1954	The Police Dog Section is established.
1965	The visits of the Royal Family, the Rolling Stones and the Beatles cause total police-leave cancellation.
1966	World Cup Football matches again cause leave cancellation.
1967	The Bootle and Liverpool Police Forces amalgamate.
1974	The Merseyside Police is formed.

APPENDIX 2 (1984)

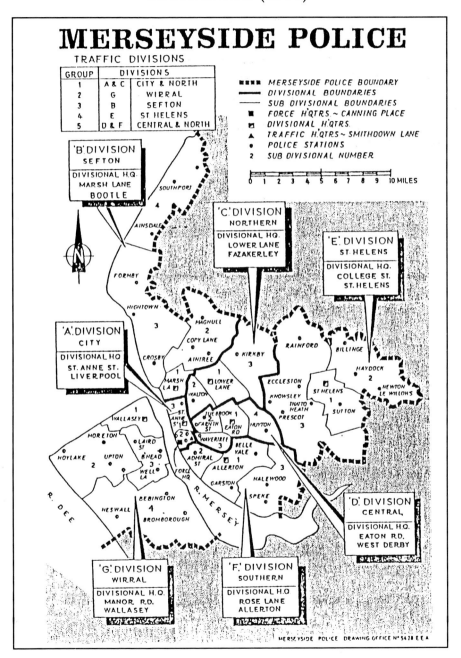

MERSEYSIDE POLICE
TRAFFIC DIVISIONS

GROUP	DIVISIONS	
1	A & C	CITY & NORTH
2	G	WIRRAL
3	B	SEFTON
4	E	ST HELENS
5	D & F	CENTRAL & NORTH

∎∎∎∎ MERSEYSIDE POLICE BOUNDARY
▬▬▬ DIVISIONAL BOUNDARIES
▬▬▬ SUB DIVISIONAL BOUNDARIES
∎ FORCE H'QTRS. ~ CANNING PLACE
▨ DIVISIONAL H'QTRS.
▲ TRAFFIC H'QTRS ~ SMITHDOWN LANE
● POLICE STATIONS
2 SUB DIVISIONAL NUMBER

0 1 2 3 4 5 6 7 8 9 10 MILES

'B' DIVISION
SEFTON
DIVISIONAL H.Q.
MARSH LANE
BOOTLE

'C' DIVISION
NORTHERN
DIVISIONAL H.Q.
LOWER LANE
FAZAKERLEY

'E' DIVISION
ST HELENS
DIVISIONAL H.Q.
COLLEGE ST.
ST. HELENS

'A' DIVISION
CITY
DIVISIONAL H.Q.
ST. ANNE ST.
LIVERPOOL

'D' DIVISION
CENTRAL
DIVISIONAL H.Q.
EATON R.D.
WEST DERBY

'G' DIVISION
WIRRAL
DIVISIONAL H.Q.
MANOR R.D.
WALLASEY

'F' DIVISION
SOUTHERN
DIVISIONAL H.Q.
ROSE LANE
ALLERTON

MERSEYSIDE POLICE DRAWING OFFICE No 5428 E E A

93

INDEX